Fatherhood Matters!

Anthony Owens

Dedication

I dedicate this book to my beloved wife, Wanda, who has stood by me through thick and thin. I am deeply grateful to her for single-handedly caring for our son during my extended deployments. In addition to providing the essential nurturing, guidance, and support expected of mothers, she also filled the void of my absence as a father.

The journey of a single parent is rife with challenges, stress, and moments of overwhelming intensity. Yet, amidst the quiet of lonely nights, there exists a resolve that transcends the darkness. For forty years, Wanda has flawlessly embodied the roles of wife and companion, weathering financial struggles and emotional turbulence with grace.

I am profoundly grateful for her steadfastness, patience, unwavering support, and boundless love.

Acknowledgment

I want to extend my heartfelt gratitude to everyone who played a part in bringing this book to life. Specifically, I would like to personally thank all those who generously shared their stories with me. Your contributions have provided invaluable support, clarity, and a deeper understanding of the significance of fatherhood.

First and foremost, I want to express my deepest appreciation to my spouse, Wanda, whose unwavering support and understanding have been my rock throughout this journey. Your love and encouragement have been my guiding light.

To my family and friends, thank you for your endless encouragement and belief in my dreams. Your support has been invaluable.

I want to express a special thank you to my TikTok family for their unwavering support and the valuable insights and personal experiences they have shared. Your contributions have played a significant role in bringing this book to fruition.

I am also grateful to my readers, whose enthusiasm and feedback continually inspire me to strive for excellence.

Thank you all for being a part of this adventure.

Author's Note

My desire to write this important and necessary book stems from my upbringing and the challenges I faced and observed during my childhood. The struggles of a single parent and the adversities they face, I witnessed them firsthand. Raised by a single mother, along with my brother and sister, I witnessed the challenges and struggles she endured and how they consumed her life, confiscating her personal time. Her existence revolved around raising her children and doing all she could to provide for us under often dire circumstances.

I wrote this book to highlight the indispensable role men play in their children's lives, prompted by my observations of numerous single-mother-led families. Even in today's modern age, the presence of fatherhood remains elusive in many households, leading to instability within the family unit. Experiencing the effects of this societal rupture during my own childhood, I have seen firsthand its profound impact on mental stability and societal progress. This book is a sincere effort to address and heal the divide, with the goal of fostering a healthier mindset for our society and future generations.

Fathers must be present and active; their absence makes a tremendous difference – both to the parent and children. As a child, being in the dark about the adults' affairs, I often blamed myself for my father's absence, questioning whether he loved me or not, why he wasn't there, and if it was my fault. Children should not have to deal with such emotional turmoil in their childhood, but sadly, they often do.

This book serves as a compass, guiding fathers to understand the roles and significance they hold within their families. While this book accentuates the importance of fatherhood, I want to be clear that women have always and continue to fulfill the role of single parents and continue to do an outstanding job. This book in no way diminishes the achievements and steadfast efforts of mothers. Throughout this book, there are many instances where the word "father or fatherhood" can easily be replaced with "mother or motherhood," as they are interchangeable in the context of single parenting.

Contents

Introduction

"'Father is the noblest title a man can be given. It is more than a biological role. It signifies a patriarch, a leader, an exemplar, a confidant, a teacher, a hero, a friend."

~ Robert L. Backman

The glimpse of dawn marks the beginning of another day, another moment illuminating the horizons of fatherhood—a timeless concept. Its meaning and understanding alter and trace an alternate yet evolved course during every different timeline. The understanding of what being a father meant differed in the past as to what it signifies today. The meaning evolved, as did the concept. Its significance—is ever-evolving.

Fatherhood—its literal meanings define it as a state of being a father. But, when unshackled from its literal boundaries, it stands as a beacon of light, illuminating a spectrum of roles and responsibilities. The responsibilities etched in this role—nurturing the kids, cultivating a bond of friendship with them to know them, forging the path for their future, and disciplining them, craft the original meaning of this concept.

Blake Masters' (What Is Fatherhood? 11 Great Dads Outline What Fatherhood Means to Them – Daily Dad – the Blog, n.d.) words regarding fatherhood visualize its true meanings; he said, "I would say that fatherhood is the ultimate challenge, the ultimate meaning, and the ultimate pleasure in life."

The concept of fatherhood transcends the boundaries of mere biological bonds. It is a bond that any father figure can adopt—it's the role of a provider, protector, mentor, and friend. For every father, its meaning varies, and its significance differs as fatherhood, above all, is a deeply personal and evolutionary journey of the bond, molded by the unique circumstances and the depth and nature of the relationship.

It's a journey beginning from the tender moments of holding a newborn for the first time to the imparting of wisdom over the years—a journey of which every step brims with love, sacrifice, and growth.

In this dimension of fatherhood lies at the core a force so subtle yet powerful enough to alter the course of a child's life—the parental influence. A parent's influence over a child's life is like a gentle breeze, but its effect is that of a storm. This force of parental influence isn't shackled by the limitations of genetics but extends beyond it, puppeteering the psychological, emotional, and social development of a child in numerous ways.

It's concealed within the laughter shared during quality time, the murmurs of reassurance in moments of uncertainty, and the wisdom, the guidance through the unpredictable turns of life. During the delicate moments of life, this influential force cultivates the mindset of a child as they look up to their parent, with aspirations flourishing in their perception.

With time passing by, the child steps into the age of adolescence—the age of uncertainty fraught with challenges, experiences, and discoveries of the unknown. Amidst this overwhelming stage of life for an adolescent child, a father's role emerges as the pillar of strength and stability—a hand of guidance in the betraying twists of the age of adolescence. A father's presence – emotional and physical – provides a sense of security and assurance, acting as the anchor that holds life together.

At the core of this labyrinth, the father guides the child with unobstructed communication, sharing life's lessons and providing unwavering support, enabling them to navigate the intricate journey of growth. Amidst the maze lie uncertain paths concerning identity, relationships, faith, self-discovery, and the future.

This book explores the dimension of fatherhood, along with its hidden and overshadowed aspects. Navigating through the bright landscape, this book will highlight some of the unheard stories and struggles of single parents and the children raised under those circumstances, serving as a medium for the children and adults to understand each other's mindsets.

It's more than a pile of words—a guide, a compass offering guidance to the fathers in moments of doubt, inspiration in moments of struggle, and hope in moments of hopelessness. I have penned the importance of parental influence, powering the reader's mind to ponder and aid in the development of relationships.

Through various chapters exploring the historical context of fatherhood, challenges faced by fathers, and their impact on crucial aspects of adolescent development, readers can gain a profound understanding of the crucial role fathers play in children's lives. These insights are complemented by practical advice, personal anecdotes, and strategies to strengthen father-child bonds amidst societal, cultural, and personal challenges.

By highlighting the significance of fatherhood and encouraging the active involvement of father figures, my aim is to foster healthier relationships, promote emotional well-being, and empower fathers to become confident, loving, and present role models for their children.

As the readers sift through the chapters of this book, they will find a versatile journey of fatherhood brimming with the aspect of joy, the pits of challenges, the luminance of its transformative powers, and the element of hope concealed in its lines.

"In the heart of every father lies the potential to shape the future—for themselves, for their children, and for the generations to come."

Part I
Understanding the Role of Fathers

Chapter 1: The Evolution of Fatherhood

The concept of fatherhood is as ancient as time itself. The journey of this concept, painted deeply into the timeline of humanity, has sifted through countless changes and revisions.

Beginning from the Stone Age, the earliest society, and evolving into today's era of modernization, the role of a father has undergone a profound transformation. Molded and forged, each era's mark of evolution in this concept reflects the changing tides of social, economic, and cultural forces.

This journey of fatherhood begins in the mists of primordial times, where roles within families were dictated by the sheer necessity of survival. These were times when the division of labor was straightforward, guided by the natural world and the unrelenting cycle of seasons. As civilizations rose from these humble beginnings, bringing forth the wonders of agriculture, writing, and law, the concept of fatherhood began to crystallize into roles that were revered and codified. Ancient philosophies pondered the virtues and responsibilities of fatherhood, embedding these ideals within the very foundations of societies.

Yet, for all its ancient roots, the root of the concept of fatherhood has been anything but static. Each era, from the glory of empires to the dark ages of turmoil and the morning of a new world, has redefined what it means to be a father. The unyielding stone tablets and papyrus scrolls gave way to the printed word, and now, in the digital age, each transition reshaped the narrative of fatherhood in its image.

This chapter warps back to the beginnings of the journey of fatherhood, a role as ancient as humanity itself, yet reborn in the ordeal of time and social change. It is a concept—an evolving concept that transcends the simple dichotomy of past and present, inviting us to explore the depths of what it means to be a father and how this foundational role continues to evolve in the face of an ever-changing world. The evolution of fatherhood is not just a historical curiosity; it is a mirror reflecting the broader evolution of human understanding, compassion, and connection.

The Historical Perspective:

The historical perspective on fatherhood is a mind-boggling maze that expands into a vast array of cultural, economic, and social landscapes across different timelines. Tracing the lineage of fatherhood from its early incarnations to the cusp of the modern era reveals not just changes in familial roles but also broader societal transformations. This journey through time offers a window into how the perceptions and responsibilities of fatherhood have been continually reshaped by the shifting sands of history.

If we peek into the hunter-gatherer societies, the role of the father depended on the structure of the tribe. Archaeologists believe that fathers who spent most of their time away from the family hunting were the minority; in most tribes, fathers were actually present most of the time. In many cases, families hunted and foraged together: men, women, and children (A Brief History of Fatherhood, 2015).

In the early agrarian societies, the role of the father was closely tied to the land and its cultivation—a need for survival in those days. Families were predominantly extended networks where multiple generations lived under one roof or in close proximity, working the land together. In these climates of life, the father's role as a provider was direct and tangible: he was often the primary source of food, shelter, and security. This era lustered the father as a figure of authority and discipline—an anchor for the survival and prosperity of the family. As societies evolved and became more stratified, the concept of fatherhood began to reflect these changes.

Warping into ancient civilizations such as Greece and Rome, the realm of fatherhood embossed not only the provision and protection of the family but also the transmission of citizenship, social status, and property. The paterfamilias in Roman society, for example, wielded extensive power over the family, embodying the law and moral guidance within the household. These roles uplifted the father's centrality in ensuring the continuity of lineage and heritage, framing fatherhood within the broader context of duty and honor.

Then came the Middle Ages—introducing new dimensions to fatherhood, influenced significantly by the Christian church. The emphasis on moral instruction and the soul's well-being permeated family life, with fathers expected to guide their children's spiritual education and moral development.

This period also saw the rise of chivalry and courtly love, which, while romanticized, began to subtly influence the emotional aspects of fatherhood, suggesting a bond that went beyond mere authority and provision to include nurturing and protection. Forming a connection beyond providence with his family. The mindset faced a shift, an emphatic seed sowed in their hearts, cultivating and forging this concept beyond the horizons of societal responsibilities.

The profound upheavals of the Industrial Revolution brought another seismic change, marking another mark of the evolution of this concept in the scrolls of the timeline. As economies moved from agrarian bases to industrial powerhouses, the nature of work changed dramatically. Fathers often found themselves working long hours in factories, distanced from the daily lives of their children and the rhythm of home life. This physical separation marked a significant transformation in the father's role from the direct, hands-on provision to a more abstract financial provider. This era highlighted the tensions between the demands of work and family, a theme that continues to resonate in discussions of fatherhood today.

The 20th century, with its wars, social movements, and technological advancements, set the stage for a radical reimagining of fatherhood. The tumultuous backdrop of world conflicts, coupled with the rising voices of women demanding equality, challenged traditional gender roles. The latter half of the century, in particular, saw a gradual but significant shift toward more engaged fatherhood, with men taking an active part in child-rearing and domestic life, reflecting broader societal changes toward gender equality and the dismantling of rigid stereotypes.

This brief exploration through history reveals that fatherhood, far from being a static concept, has always been a fluid and evolving role shaped by the economic, social, and cultural currents of its time. Each era has left its imprint, contributing layers of complexity to the understanding of what it means to be a father. As we delve deeper into the pools of history, it becomes evident that the core of the concept of fatherhood transcends the provision and protection, touching the very heart of human connection, legacy, and love.

Modern Era Changes:

Stepping forward from the mists of the past to the shores of the present, the concept and narrative of fatherhood sprout. The shade of its presence draped in the hues of modernity, yet its roots hold the essence of its ancient roots—illuminating it as a timeless concept. The social landscape of the modern world, amidst the galloping technological advancements and the relentless pursuit of gender equality, has evolved the concept of fatherhood, reimagining its core and evolving the climate of its realm with the drizzle of emotions and responsibilities mixed in it.

In this current era, the role of a father liberates from the conventional archetypes of provider and protector. With the emotional hue mixed in its core, it morphs into a versatile identity that embraces emotional nurturing, active parenting, and an equal share in the chemistry of household responsibilities.

This evolution, this transformation, is not merely a change in duties but a significant change in the core, in the morality of fatherhood—a reflection of the society that values emotional depth, shared responsibilities, and the dismantling of rigid gender roles that had been solidified through ages of societal norms and cultures.

Today's father is no longer the sole anchor in the narrative of child-rearing, but now, standing shoulder to shoulder with the mother, he relishes and shares the joys, challenges, and sleepless nights that come with parenting. Unlike the fathers from the primordial eras, the emotion of care and empathy flares within today's father's heart. He is just as likely to be found at school meetings as he is at the boardroom table.

The evolved mental aptitude and emotional horizons made them adept at treading the narrow path of balance between professional aspirations and familial commitments. This era has witnessed the rise of stay-at-home dads, single fathers, and those championing the cause of paternity leave—every single action signaling the ripple of evolution in societal attitudes toward fatherhood and family dynamics.

Venturing forward, digitalization has paved new paths— allowing the light of fatherhood to illuminate and develop further by connecting fathers to their children through the ethereal strands of the internet, enabling them to be present in their children's lives in ways that were unimaginable just a generation ago.

But as they say, every light casts a shadow. And the shadow for this is the elimination of the human connection in the digitized world. This connectedness between a parent and child gives birth to its own set of challenges and dilemmas—navigating the pitfalls of social media to maintaining the core of human connection in this world.

Though today's concept of fatherhood stands as the fruition of its evolution from the beginning of humanity, it's also marked by a growing recognition of the psychological and emotional well-being of fathers themselves. The stoic, unflappable façade of the past is giving space to a more in-depth understanding. The perspective acknowledges that fathers, too, need support, understanding, and sometimes, healing. With this acknowledgment, the doors to new dialogues about mental health, vulnerability, and the strength embedded in seeking help further enrich the concept of fatherhood.

Peeking through the centuries and years of history, as the world stands amidst the complexities and possibilities of the modern world, the evolution of fatherhood continues to unfurl— a testament to the unending journey of human adaptation and growth.

This chapter of evolution in the concept of fatherhood is being penned every day. Not just in the ledgers of academia but in the quiet moments of bedtime stories, the chaotic mornings of school runs, and the tender embraces of warmth that speaks of love unspoken.

The story of fatherhood is a vibrant one; each aspect, every path, and every timeline is filled with change, resilience, and a deeper understanding of what it means to nurture, teach, and love.

Chapter 2: Benefits of Fatherhood

This world, this life, is like a journey through a scorching desert. Every step brings a new trial. To stay sane and find your way, you need a compass to guide you and shade to offer relief.

Amidst this journey of trepidations, the role of a father emerges as that sturdy shade tree and compass, curated from their extensive experiences, guiding their child through this desert of life.

But being a father is easy; anyone can assume that role, but nurturing its true meaning—being that shade and the beacon of guidance in the child's life is what makes a 'Father' a 'Dad.'

From the beginning of life, from their first breath, a child forms an inexplicable bond with their father. He's seen as a role model for them to follow. Unconsciously, a child absorbs the ways of their father in their habits and their personality. For a girl, the behavior and personality of her father in the house or in society become her model as she looks for those qualities in men when she's old enough to date. If the father nurtures a gentle and loving personality, the daughter will often set those traits for her choice in men.

Meanwhile, boys are often drawn to the personality of their father. They inherit that by looking up to him. At every step in life, they frequently seek their father's approval; this unquenched thirst for making their father proud lingers within them throughout life.

As human beings, we arrive in this world untamed with no understanding of the ways of the world. But we bring with us the ability to perceive. From the early steps of life, a child begins to imitate and understand the ways of life by analyzing the ways of people around them. They come into the world as a blank canvas, and as they step up the ladder of age, the canvas begins to be painted in different shades.

Without a father in their life, children may struggle to understand the world around them and might walk a path without knowing whether it's right or wrong. They might be vulnerable—both emotionally and mentally. But a father's presence helps to purge those vulnerabilities from them. With a role model in their house, it is often unlikely for children to seek inspiration from the outside world.

A father serves as the anchor that holds a child's life together, keeping everything in place. When a father is consistently present in a child's routine, it naturally instills a sense of caution and guidance in their life.

A father would often lay down rules and enforce them, and the child would navigate their life with those rules in mind. Whenever they find themselves at a junction, and the wrong path allures them, the echoes of those rules and the fear of their father's disappointment may make them hesitate before choosing.

When the true meaning of fatherhood is cultivated by the father, when he becomes that shade in their lives, it nourishes their soul, molding their personality and forging the path toward a destination that brims with respect and humanity—crafting their inner growth and strength.

Emotional Benefits:

The history of fatherhood traces the evolution of this role over the centuries, showing how it transformed from being simply a provider and enforcer of rules in the household to becoming deeply involved in the emotional development of the child. Decades ago, many fathers were entrenched in traditional notions of masculinity, characterized by imposing strict rules, using physical discipline, and unintentionally creating an emotional void in their children. This lack of emotional intelligence resulted in a narrow and limited perspective on society, hindering children's ability to understand and appreciate the world's diversity, including different beliefs and personalities. Consequently, narrow-mindedness flourished, whereas open-mindedness could have been nurtured.

In contrast, in today's world, journeying through the ages of time, the concept of fatherhood has evolved, and the core concept of emotional support has sprouted in it.

Security and Safety:

There are moments in life when it feels like the world is against you. The journey can be exhausting, and that weariness can create a deep sense of vulnerability. Everything can seem empty and hopeless. In these times, the father's role shines as a beacon of light in the darkness, offering security and hope when it's needed most.

Even the smallest gestures, like a pat on the back or a few encouraging words, can make a child feel secure when they come from a father. These acts serve as a shield against the hardships of the world and offer hope in times of despair. A father, having experienced similar challenges, can frequently recognize the signs of stress in a child's behavior and offers emotional support, providing a comforting blanket of security and safety.

Emotional Support:

A father's emotional support provides stability and grounding in a child's life, giving them the strength to overcome life's obstacles. Sometimes, the weight of worries and fears can stifle the courage needed to move forward, making even the smallest step feel like an insurmountable challenge. But an emotionally aware father brings warmth and reassurance into the child's life. He is there when they need him most, listening to their heartaches and helping to lift the burdens that weigh them down.

This attentive listening makes the child feel heard and teaches them to value their emotions, providing a secure platform for them to express their feelings. Continuous communication and the validation children receive from their fathers build trust, strengthening their bond over time.

Among the many benefits that a father's emotional support brings to a child, one stands out most vividly: the development of resilience and patience. A father fosters these qualities by encouraging a growth mindset, motivating the child to embrace new challenges, explore uncharted territories in life, and enrich their experiences with courage and bravery.

Typically, a person hesitates to venture into the unknown or unfamiliar. However, an emotionally supportive father encourages them to take that step, pushing them out of their comfort zones. He helps cultivate the courage needed to face challenges head-on rather than shy away from them.

This might involve allowing them to tackle a problem on their own, confront a specific fear, or manage a difficult task. While it may feel uncomfortable for the child at the time, a father understands the bigger picture—he sees his child learning to handle frustrations and failures, all while developing resilience and determination.

Throughout this journey, a father's presence acts as a comforting shade, offering a sense of stability and reassurance during the child's developmental phase. The child feels secure, knowing they are not alone and have a supportive figure who truly cares for them. This reassuring presence fosters the courage to face uncertain situations while easing anxiety and stress. Rather than leaving the child to face challenges alone, a father provides affirmation through his words, shaping the child's mind, instilling self-respect, and building a positive self-image.

Another crucial aspect of a child's emotional growth comes from a father's willingness to share his own life experiences. This opens a gateway for the child to learn how to express their own experiences as well. Listening to their father's stories of facing challenges and overcoming them can ignite the child's mind with insights on managing emotions and dealing with difficulties. The father becomes a real-life hero in their eyes, planting a seed of inspiration as the child aspires to follow in his footsteps.

A father's willingness to be open about his emotions can deeply influence a child's emotional intelligence. When he shares his joy, sadness, or fears, he helps his child explore their own emotions, imparting valuable lessons on understanding and managing feelings. This emotional awareness becomes an essential tool throughout the child's life, enhancing their ability to connect with others and build meaningful relationships.

By breaking down communication barriers, a father offers a unique emotional blueprint that helps a child understand the world and their role within it. Amid the complex emotions of growing up, a father's influence shines through the stories he shares and the values he instills, enriching the child's emotional landscape and equipping them to navigate their own journey with empathy and insight.

Social Benefits:

Beyond the emotional benefits, fatherhood also plays a crucial role in shaping a child's social life. Fathers become pillars of support, enriching a child's social experiences through their presence. Through both direct and indirect interactions, they help develop essential social skills and a deeper understanding of the world, guiding the child in navigating lifelong relationships and societal interactions.

A father's engagement often introduces a child to the broader social world through community activities, sports, cultural events, and school events. This exposure is invaluable, as it teaches children how to navigate various social situations and understand different social cues and norms. Through these experiences, children learn the importance of teamwork, the value of cooperation, and the skills needed for conflict resolution. The child experiences the world firsthand under the shade of his father, giving them the freedom to submerge themselves in society—absorb the good and avoid the bad. This adaptability is crucial for personal and professional success, enabling children to feel comfortable and perform well in diverse settings.

A father's communication style and approach to solving problems can deeply influence a child's ability to communicate effectively with others. For example, a father who uses negotiation and compromise in resolving conflicts at home will teach his children to employ similar strategies in their own interactions. This ability to communicate effectively and resolve disputes is invaluable in building and maintaining lasting relationships.

Fathers often introduce a sense of challenge and encouragement that drives children to explore new experiences and reach beyond their usual limits, promoting social courage and resilience. Whether it's encouraging a shy child to join a sports team or supporting a teenager through the trials of making new friends after a move, a father's push can help a child overcome social anxieties and build confidence in their abilities to connect with others.

Socialization within the family unit itself, especially in families where multiple generations interact regularly, also plays a crucial role. Fathers who facilitate and encourage these multigenerational interactions help children understand respect, empathy, and the nature of interpersonal dynamics across different age groups. This understanding is especially significant in today's age-diverse workplaces and communities. Fatherhood's branches spread further into the role modeling fathers provide in their daily lives, whether interacting with neighbors, colleagues, or family friends, setting a real-world example of how to manage and nurture relationships.

Children who see their fathers actively maintaining and cherishing friendships learn the importance of investing in relationships themselves. The social networks that fathers contribute to their children's lives are platforms for developing interpersonal skills and serve as safety nets that provide support, advice, and opportunities. These networks can lead to internships, careers, and partnerships, proving instrumental in the child's future success.

Through various dimensions of social interaction and modeling, fathers equip their children with the tools to navigate the complexities of social relationships and obligations. This comprehensive social education helps children grow into well-rounded, socially experienced adults capable of contributing positively and effectively to their communities and society at large.

Fatherhood in Cognitive Development:

Fatherhood plays a crucial role in the cognitive development of a child, serving as a catalyst for intellectual growth through diverse and dynamic interactions. When a father engages actively in his child's learning processes from infancy through adolescence, he contributes significantly to the expansion of the child's cognitive abilities. From the earliest days of a child's life, when a father reads bedtime stories, he is not just lulling his child to sleep but also stimulating language acquisition and auditory processing skills. This routine nurtures a love for reading and an early grasp of language, laying the foundation for later literacy skills in the child.

Moreover, the questions and discussions that arise from these stories encourage children to think critically and creatively, sparking their imagination and curiosity. As the child grows, a father's involvement often extends to educational activities like building models, solving puzzles, or exploring the outdoors. These activities are not mere pastimes; they are critical in developing problem-solving skills and understanding the physical world. For example, a father helping his child calculate the angles for a perfect basketball shot subtly introduces concepts of geometry and physics.

Venturing further into the role of fatherhood, a sight emerges of fathers who introduce concepts such as numbers, shapes, and logic through play. Though, on the outside, those might seem like regular activities, but in-depth, they are setting the stage for mathematical literacy and logical reasoning skills in the child's mind-expanding aptitude. The hands-on approach helps demystify abstract concepts, making them more tangible and understandable for young minds. This method of learning through doing not only deepens a child's comprehension but also enhances their ability to apply knowledge in real-world scenarios.

The gates of communication have always been the vitality of a father-child relationship, birthing and nurturing an array of qualities in the child. Fathers who encourage exploration and questioning foster an environment where cognitive skills can flourish. This encouragement is crucial for developing critical thinking skills. By challenging their children to think about 'why' and 'how' rather than just 'what,' fathers promote a deeper understanding and a critical approach to information that is essential in today's information-rich world.

In discussions, fathers often encourage their children to express their thoughts clearly and justify their opinions. This dialogue serves as a bridge toward the enhancement of cognitive flexibility and verbal skills. It also teaches children how to structure their thoughts coherently and argue their points logically, skills that are invaluable in academic and professional settings.

The emotional support a father provides is intrinsically linked to cognitive development. Children who feel secure are more likely to take intellectual risks, such as tackling difficult problems or creative endeavors. The confidence instilled by a supportive father enables a child to engage fully with cognitive challenges without fear of failure.

Thus, fatherhood, through its varied interactions and engagements, significantly molds and enhances a child's cognitive development. This complex interplay of emotional support, intellectual stimulation, and real-world application equips children with the necessary tools to navigate an increasingly complex world, ensuring they not only accumulate knowledge but are also adept at using it effectively.

A Father's Role in Nurturing:

The nurturing role of fathers, often seen as complementary to that of mothers, plays an indispensable part in the healthy development of a child. Historically, the father's role has been characterized by providing and protecting, but modern understanding appreciates that fathers nurture in distinctive and essential ways that profoundly affect a child's emotional and psychological well-being.

Nowadays, a father's involvement is marked not just by the provision of comfort and care but also by fostering independence and resilience.

Through various forms of interaction—playing sports, engaging in physical activities, or even participating in everyday tasks—fathers often encourage their children to push their limits and test their strengths. This approach significantly aids in building self-confidence and self-reliance, crucial attributes for personal development.

Fathers often infuse their parenting with a unique sense of adventure. Whether it's discovering a new park, fishing on a lake, or tackling a new DIY project at home, these activities make learning both fun and hands-on. Through these experiences, children learn to be curious, to ask questions, and to embrace learning by doing.

In the realm of discipline, fathers often bring a unique perspective. They tend to enforce boundaries in a manner that promotes independence and responsibility. By being firm yet fair, fathers help children understand the consequences of their actions and the importance of maintaining integrity and respect for others.

Fathers who manifest the true meaning of fatherhood contribute to the nurturing environment of the family by supporting and respecting the co-parenting role, demonstrating to children the importance of partnership, cooperation, and mutual respect within the family unit. This collaborative approach not only strengthens the family bond but also models social and interpersonal skills necessary for life outside the home.

"The difference between a 'man' and a 'father' is that the former shares his genes, but the latter gives his life."

~ Craig D. Lounsbrough

Chapter 3: Challenges Faced by Fathers

Fatherhood, while rich with rewards, is fraught with its own unique set of challenges.

The path of a father is often steep and rugged, laden with societal expectations and personal trials that test the limits of their resilience and strength.

There are moments in the life of those who walk down the path of true fatherhood that may become obscured, posing a threat to their indefinite love and care for their children. Hidden—sometimes in the form of work, sometimes in the guise of limited choices, but the threats are persistent, especially for the fathers who tread down this path alone without a partner sharing the burden of responsibilities.

Throughout the history of this concept, these dangers and threats have always been present. Now, as we approach the dawn of a new era, these fears continue to cast a shadow over this journey. One of the underlying causes of these challenges is grasping the concept of parenthood. Whether it is the role of a mother or a father, both face this trial as they venture into the parenting world.

As humans, it's natural for us to learn through the lens of perception. From the earliest moments of childhood, our journey of learning starts by observing and absorbing the knowledge reflected in the actions of those around us, especially our parents.

Most children who grow up to be parents learn the art of parenting through the perception of their parents' nurturing style. A daughter would curate the idea of how she should be treated by seeing how her father treats her mother, and similarly, a boy would learn the value of a woman through his father's actions. The same phenomena apply to the art of parenting—when to pamper, when to show patience, and when and how to discipline a child.

For parents who grew up without having role models to guide them, stepping into the role of parenthood can feel like navigating in the dark. The prospect of becoming a parent is often daunting, and for those who lack parental figures, their understanding of parenting is shaped by observing society—like how their friend's father treated them, for instance. This learning process can lead them in either direction—right or wrong—depending on who they observe and learn from.

In other cases, being raised by a single parent may have limited their emotional experience to just one side of the spectrum. Without the chance to develop the skills needed for building deep bonds, they may feel uncertain about how to maintain a strong relationship. This fear can sometimes drive them to compensate by showering their children with gifts and toys, leaving the children deprived of the essential blessing of genuine communication.

Facing these challenges on the journey of fatherhood presents a trial that cannot be easily overcome. One must navigate the pressures that bear down on them, whether from societal expectations or their own fears of inadequacy, stemming from a lack of exposure to such experiences.

Navigating the Tides of Expectation:

In society, fathers are often perceived as the bedrock of the family, expected to provide stability, discipline, and financial support. Fathers were and are expected to be unyielding and unemotional as history dictated their role, but with the evolution of this concept, they are now required to be equally nurturing and present, too. The duality of these expectations can create an internal struggle as they balance their role within the family against societal norms that often do not allow for openness.

The journey of a father is deeply influenced by the choppy waters of societal expectations, where every ripple brings a challenge of balancing traditional roles with evolving demands. These expectations, often deeply ingrained, serve as both a guide and a formidable obstacle, shaping how a father perceives his duties and how he is perceived by others.

Cultural Legacy and the Modern Shift:

Traditionally, fathers have been viewed primarily as stoic, strong, and always in control. However, as society evolves, so too does the concept of fatherhood. Today's fathers are expected to not only be providers but also active participants in their children's emotional and physical care. They are encouraged to be sensitive, nurturing, and accessible—traits traditionally ascribed to mothers.

This shift, while positive, introduces a complex set of challenges. Fathers now may find themselves needing to excel in roles that they may not have witnessed from their own fathers. The pressure to conform to this maze of expectations can be overwhelming, especially when their own upbringing and societal influences continue to glorify the traditional, stoic male figure.

The Pressure to Perform:

The expectation for fathers to excel as both providers and parents can be a challenging burden, testing their patience and determination. In the workplace, they are expected to push their limits, often prioritizing career growth to fulfill the provider role effectively. At the same time, modern parenting standards require fathers to be actively engaged at home—attending school meetings, participating in childcare, and being emotionally available to their children and partners.

Balancing these dual expectations can lead to internal conflicts and the building up of stress. Many fathers struggle with guilt and anxiety over not spending enough time with their families due to work commitments, as the roots of guilt undermine their determination.

On the other hand, when they prioritize family, they may face criticism from peers or superiors who uphold traditional work-first values. Every decision and every action they take puts them to the test, with society's judgment on one side and their family's needs on the other.

Stigma and Isolation:

Amid these challenges, the stigma around discussing struggles or seeking help remains a significant barrier. The fear of judgment for not living up to these idealized standards prevents many fathers from expressing vulnerabilities or discussing their parenting insecurities. This lack of open dialogue can lead to isolation, as fathers may feel they are the only ones struggling to meet these divided expectations.

As they continue, the societal reluctance to fully accept emotional expression in men creates an environment where fathers' mental health can suffer without adequate support or recognition. This silence surrounding the challenges of fatherhood perpetuates a cycle of stress and isolation, making it even harder for fathers to navigate the expectations placed upon them.

For example, a Black father may find his life overshadowed by negative stereotypes and low expectations. Society often fails to recognize him as a potential role model for his children, instead associating him with the worst societal ills. This kind of discrimination, which can affect fathers of any ethnicity, can create significant obstacles for a father who might otherwise be an excellent parent. However, the mounting stress from such biases can weaken his resolve.

To better support fathers in navigating these high seas of expectations, society must cultivate an environment where men feel safe to express vulnerabilities and discuss their challenges without fear of judgment or ridicule. By advocating for realistic, flexible views of fatherhood that allow men to define their paternal roles more freely, we can begin to dismantle the barriers that keep fathers from fully embracing both the joys and trials of fatherhood. Only then can we ensure that fathers are supported as they strive to meet the complex and rewarding demands of modern parenting.

The Tightrope of Work-Life Integration:

Treading upon the tightrope of work-life integration is a significant challenge for fathers in today's society, where the demands of the modern work environment often exceed the traditional 9-to-5 schedule. Increased responsibilities, expectations of constant availability, and competitive cultures extend work hours and encroach on family time. Technology exacerbates this by allowing work to follow fathers home, blurring the lines between professional and personal life.

The psychological impact of these demands is substantial, with fathers experiencing chronic stress, potential burnout, and even depression as they struggle to fulfill dual roles effectively. This ongoing stress can make fathers physically present but mentally distracted at home, leading to feelings of guilt and inadequacy. The effects on family life are profound. Children and partners may feel neglected, and the family dynamic can suffer, potentially affecting children's emotional and developmental health.

Unique Troubles Faced by Single Fathers:

Single fathers often grapple with societal stereotypes that do not traditionally associate men with solo parenting. This bias can manifest in various aspects of their daily lives, from interactions with schools and healthcare providers to their own social circles, where they may feel isolated or scrutinized. Additionally, single fathers frequently encounter legal and institutional hurdles that can complicate custody arrangements, access to child support, and fair treatment in family courts. The dilemma of Dwayne, a father who is co-parenting, resonates with many of the fathers out there. He described to me the difficulties he faces due to his unique situation. Despite his desire to actively participate in his daughter's life, he encounters resistance from her mother. This leads him to frequent court battles in pursuit of visitation rights, and he has even attempted to gain full custody, though unsuccessfully. Currently, he is seeking additional legal support in his quest for joint or full custody. Dwyane expressed, "Whenever I have the chance to spend time with my little angel, the world seems to stand still." He added, "I will continue to do everything in my power to see my daughter."

The emotional toll on single fathers can be substantial. They must deal with their own emotional needs while fully attending to those of their children, often having to suppress their feelings to maintain a facade of strength. This emotional juggling act can lead to increased stress, anxiety, and, in some cases, depression.

Single fathers might also deal with financial challenges as the sole provider. They face the dual pressure of meeting all household expenses and fulfilling the role of both parents, which can lead to longer working hours and less time spent with their children. The absence of a secondary income also means any financial setback can have immediate and severe consequences for the family's stability.

Fostering a Supportive Environment for Fathers:

Recognizing the challenges faced by fathers is only the first step in creating a nurturing environment that allows them to thrive both at home and in their professional lives. Encouraging open dialogue about the realities of fatherhood can help break down the stigmas associated with paternal sensitivity. In this journey of cultivating a path of support for fathers, society needs to understand that each human, no matter what ethnicity, is unique in their own ways, undefined by the actions of others. By reframing the narrative to recognize that fathers, like all parents, need support and understanding, we can start to relieve some of the pressures they endure.

Achieving a better balance requires both individual and systemic efforts. Fathers can set boundaries with employers, define specific work hours, and make a conscious effort to disconnect from work during family time. Systemic changes are also needed in the workplace, such as flexible working arrangements like telecommuting, compressed work weeks, and a culture that values efficiency over long hours. Society's role is also crucial. Redefining successful fatherhood to include active involvement at home and recognizing the importance of fathers' roles beyond being providers can help reduce the stigma that compels fathers to prioritize work over family.

Addressing the work-life balance challenge for fathers involves a combination of personal resolve, supportive workplace policies, and a societal shift in perceptions of fatherhood and male responsibilities in family life.

Community support groups and resources also emerge as one of the pillars in the navigation of the trials of fatherhood. Among the various strategies fathers can use to maintain their mental well-being, seeking mental health support specifically designed for them stands out as a vital choice. This support helps them manage stress and develop coping strategies that enhance their overall well-being.

Among the various aspects of this concept, the challenges faced by a single father stand out as the most turbulent. Fathers occupy a unique position in parenting, facing a distinct set of challenges that require both resilience and creativity. The journey of a single father is marked by navigating the demands of parenthood alone, often without the support systems or societal recognition afforded to single mothers.

Understanding these challenges is the first step in empowering single fathers to thrive while fostering strong, healthy relationships with their children.

Strategies to Overcome Challenges for Single Fathers

Building a Support Network:

One of the most effective ways single fathers can tackle the challenges they face is by building a robust support network. This can include family members, friends, and other single parents who can offer practical help and emotional support. Community resources such as parenting classes and counseling services can also provide necessary guidance and a sense of community.

They can join support groups exclusively for single fathers whose lives are burdened by overwhelming responsibilities that can suffocate their resolve to care for their children. Being surrounded by others in similar situations may help them find their way toward a more stable life with their children. Participating in these groups, especially those made up of single fathers, offers a safe space to express concerns, share experiences, and receive advice and encouragement from peers who truly understand their struggles.

Prioritizing Self-Care:

Navigating the challenges of single fatherhood demands both physical and emotional resilience. Fathers must prioritize their well-being by engaging in regular exercise, getting enough sleep, eating healthy, and seeking mental health support when necessary. By practicing self-care, they can maintain their health and well-being, which is crucial for being fully present and actively involved in their children's lives.

Establishing Routines:

Stability is crucial for children, especially in single-parent families. Single fathers can foster a sense of security and normalcy by establishing consistent daily routines. This includes set times for meals, homework, activities, and bedtime. Routines not only help children feel secure but also help fathers manage their time and responsibilities more effectively.

Embracing Open Communication:

Open and honest communication between fathers and their children is vital. Fathers should encourage their children to express their feelings and thoughts, which can help strengthen the parent-child relationship and provide emotional relief for both parties. This open dialogue also helps fathers identify and address any issues their children may be facing.

The path of single fatherhood, while cluttered with challenges, also offers immense opportunities for personal growth and deepening familial bonds. By actively seeking support, managing their well-being, and fostering open communication, fathers can tackle the challenges they face and create a nurturing environment where their children can thrive.

All in all, the journey of fatherhood, with all its trials and tribulations, is one of profound significance. By addressing societal expectations and work-life challenges and supporting fathers in their role, people can contribute to a healthier, more balanced approach to parenting. Fathers who feel supported and understood are better equipped to raise happy, healthy children and contribute positively to their communities.

As we delve deeper into this concept, a clear truth emerges from the challenges that define fatherhood: it is a role shaped not only by strength but also by courage, compassion, and vulnerability.

Part II
Fathers and Their Impact on Adolescence

Chapter 4: Identity Development

From the earliest stages of life, as the human psyche begins to form, we learn the subtleties of life through perception. This journey of learning improves significantly when an individual identifies a role model to guide them.

It's in human nature to select a role model based on qualities they feel they lack and what they aspire to become.

For many children, role models change as they grow, ranging from cartoon characters to real-life figures. However, what remains constant throughout the ages is the perception of a father as the ultimate role model.

Fathers as Role Models:

From the pregnancy stage onward, a father's behavior and treatment of the mother play a crucial role in the child's neurological development. Even before birth, the child's subconscious is active and deeply connected to the mother's consciousness, absorbing and internalizing the emotions she experiences.

As children enter the world, a mother shapes their emotional development, while a father takes on the role of a guiding figure. Every action, word, behavior, and emotional expression of the father is absorbed by the child and imprinted in their subconscious as life lessons, serving as a roadmap for navigating the world and reflecting the influence of their role model.

Throughout history, regardless of their level of involvement in the family, fathers have consistently been regarded as the primary role models for their children. Even during the medieval era, when fathers were often preoccupied with wars and conquests, their physical absence did not lessen their influence. Children still looked up to them, striving to emulate their actions and principles.

A father seeks to embody his warrior spirit, with his child standing beside him, ready to defend their land and earn recognition for their abilities. Such aspirations were common even in bygone eras, where fathers were revered as the primary role models for their children. While this drive was most often seen in sons, daughters were inspired by their fathers' bravery and felt the same urge to join the battle.

In today's unpredictable world, where children are especially vulnerable to outside influences, a father's role as a role model goes beyond just setting an example; it also involves providing emotional guidance.

The enduring ideal of true fatherhood requires fathers to act as a guiding light for their children, helping them navigate the emotional challenges of modern society. Psychological research revealed that when children observed their father to be physically and verbally aggressive toward a plastic Bobo doll, the chances of them manifesting those qualities were significantly higher, as the children would often mimic their actions if given the opportunity. (Why Fathers Are Important Role Models for Boys, 2013).

Effects of a Father's Presence and Absence:

Having a father figure in a child's life is crucial, as he becomes the primary figure of admiration. The skills a father can cultivate in a child through his role modeling differ from those imparted by mothers, and it's vital to appreciate and honor these distinctions.

A father figure engages children in lively activities, injecting fun into their lives while also teaching them to channel aggression constructively. Through various sports such as soccer or basketball, fathers instill values of good sportsmanship in their children, guiding them through societal pressures and fueling their ambition to push beyond their boundaries.

As children progress through the stages of life under the influence of a father figure, they absorb qualities like integrity, honesty, and reliability by observing the coalition between their father's words and actions, whether in social interactions or domestic affairs.

Coupled with these attributes, a genuine father figure instills in children the importance of emotional expression, encouraging them to openly display both positive and negative feelings. This guidance assists children in navigating emotional challenges and communicating effectively.

As a role model, a father embodies the image of an unwavering individual who remains steadfast in his commitments, whether they pertain to his professional obligations or other responsibilities. He exhibits resilience in the face of challenges and adeptly resolves problems as they arise. By showcasing these qualities, he instills in the child a sense of prioritization, fostering accountability and diligence in their conduct. Moreover, he imparts the significance of maintaining optimism and determination when confronted with obstacles. However, the absence of a father figure leaves a void in the lives of children—a void where a reliable role model should be present.

The absence of a guiding figure in their daily lives means children may miss the chance to learn essential qualities like decency and respect, leaving room for less positive influences to fill that gap. In their search for guidance, a child might look up to an older student at school or an older person in the neighborhood, unintentionally adopting them as role models.

Though they may seem mature to children, these individuals are still in the process of shaping their own identities and facing life's challenges, which can sometimes lead them astray. When children observe negative behaviors, such as smoking, drinking, or displaying weakness in the face of adversity, they may unknowingly adopt these undesirable traits. For example, if children see their perceived role models, like older peers, being respected by others or involved in a gang, they may mistakenly believe that these behaviors are essential for earning respect.

Psychology Today presents the research conducted regarding the results of a father's absence, exploring each aspect where it impacts the children's life, such as diminished self-concept, compromised physical and emotional security, behavioral problems, truancy and poor academic performance, and more (A Father's Impact on Child Development, 2018). Each of these factors adds to the instability in a child's life, overshadowing their future prospects.

History of African American Fathers and Its Impacts:

Since the colonial era of the late 1700s, the institution of racial slavery became deeply entrenched in American society. Black individuals were deprived of their identities as parents and endured the cruelty inflicted by their "owners." This enduring concept profoundly shaped the collective mindset of their race.

Today, while racism is more openly acknowledged and condemned than it was centuries ago, the enduring effects of familial separation continue to resonate within the lives and thoughts of Black families. The legacy of disrupted fatherhood traces back to the colonial era, where many children in Black households grew up without the presence of fathers, creating a lasting sense of distance within families.

This injustice against the Black community has rippled through centuries, marking a significant effect in the 1960s. In 1964, President Lyndon Johnson launched a war against poverty in America. A war that destabilized the slowly stabilizing Black families – disrupting their family mechanics. Project 21's Christopher Arps (LBJ's "War on Poverty" Hurt Black Americans, 2014) highlighted this fact in his statement regarding the poverty war; he said:

"Roughly 75 percent of black children were born to a married two-parent family when the 'war' began in 1964. By 2008, the percentage of black babies born out of wedlock numbered over 72 percent. Today, the rate of unwed motherhood in the black community is more than twice as high as among whites — and almost three times higher than before big government's grand intervention..."

The very next year of the war, in 1965, Patrick Moynihan published "The Moynihan Report" (BlackPast, 2007) that shed light upon the factors that ruptured the Black families' mechanism, addressing the problems sprouting due to it.

- The institution of American slavery robbed individuals of their dignity, completely depriving them of societal protection and reducing enslaved Black Americans to mere "chattel."

- After emancipation, former slaves gained freedom but faced widespread inequality. Black males encountered hostility and endured public humiliation due to Jim Crow segregation laws. Any attempt to resist often resulted in the threat of lynching. The once-respected image of the strong Black father figure was systematically degraded.

- The rapid urbanization as Black individuals transitioned from Southern agricultural settings to Northern cities put significant strain on existing social structures.

- Unemployment and reliance on welfare services often placed case workers, predominantly women, in direct communication with mothers. This dynamic sometimes fueled resentment from fathers who felt marginalized, as the involvement of two women in family matters diminished his perceived authority as the household head. Economically disadvantaged Black families often have more children and lower median incomes, which makes it necessary for the wife to seek employment outside the home.

- Success for men is frequently gauged by their income. Black fathers often earn less than their white counterparts, leading to feelings of insecurity and occasionally diminishing respect from their spouses.

• Black women frequently assumed the role of family matriarch, which diminished the presence of male fathers and weakened their influence on the character development of children.

• Economic hardship, lack of opportunities, and social isolation contributed to higher rates of delinquency and crime among Black males.

• A disproportionate number of crimes are attributed to Black males. A criminal record complicates employment prospects and can lead to the revocation of voting rights, exacerbating the challenges faced by Black males.

The historical injustice endured by the Black community has resulted in a significant absence of fathers in the lives of children, a legacy that persists into our present era. The repercussions of this disruption continue to affect our society, with too many Black men being deprived of their parental roles due to the systemic treatment and portrayal they have faced. According to the Office for National Statistics, Black parents with dependent children are more likely to be single than any other ethnic group (Harker, 2019).

It's like a domino effect—once one-piece falls, it causes the others to topple as well. The absence of a father figure in the lives of some Black children often drives them toward the streets, where they look up to others who have faced similar struggles, perpetuating the cycle.

The absence of father figures acts as a malignant force, permeating the lives of children, particularly during their vulnerable adolescent years when they are most susceptible to the world's challenges. The absence of a father's presence can undermine the emotional and social development of Black children, potentially stripping away essential qualities needed for their growth. This void can leave them vulnerable, often leading them to seek guidance from individuals who may become negative role models.

Identity Development:

Identity development during adolescence is a complex and dynamic process where young individuals craft their self-concept and navigate their place in the world. Fathers play a pivotal role in this process by influencing their children's beliefs, behaviors, and self-perception. The presence of a father in a child's life often enhances their confidence and self-worth.

Father figures provide both implicit and explicit feedback about their children's capabilities and values, influencing how they see themselves and their potential. For example, when a father actively participates in a child's education or extracurricular activities, it not only boosts the child's confidence in those areas but also in their general ability to achieve goals. This support helps solidify the child's self-concept as capable and valued, which is critical during the fragile adolescent years.

The support and encouragement provided by fathers to their children nurture their confidence, empowering them to explore diverse interests and hobbies. These experiences play a crucial role in shaping their identity development. This encouragement enables adolescents to explore different roles, ultimately choosing those that resonate most with their personal identity. Whether it's sports, arts, or academic endeavors, the supportive guidance from a father empowers children to follow their passions and cultivate a unique sense of self.

The presence of a father figure also plays a prominent role in the moral and ethical development of their children by modeling values such as honesty, integrity, and respect. These values become integral components of the child's identity. Adolescents learn to internalize these values through consistent observation of their father's actions and the discussions that follow those observations. Through the lens of this guidance, their minds form a moral compass that could steer their decisions and behaviors throughout life. With a robust sense of self-development nurtured by positive paternal influence, adolescents are more adept at resisting negative peer pressure.

Fathers who engage in open communication with their children about life's challenges, including those encountered within peer groups, equip their offspring to make independent and thoughtful decisions. This resilience plays a pivotal role in shaping identity and empowering children to steadfastly uphold their values and beliefs even in the face of adversity. It strengthens their convictions with the armor of patience, gradually tempering impulsiveness and enabling them to approach debates, arguments, or confrontations with rationality and composure.

The absence of a father figure can significantly disrupt an adolescent's identity development, introducing challenges that may persist throughout their life. In such situations, adolescents often seek alternative male figures to fill the paternal void. This pursuit can be beneficial if they encounter positive role models who provide guidance and stability. However, if they turn to unsuitable individuals, it may lead to the adoption of negative behaviors. These surrogate figures can profoundly influence their evolving identity, either positively or negatively.

Without a father's stabilizing influence, adolescents may become more vulnerable to negative influences that offer to fill the emotional or psychological void. This vulnerability can result in compromised decision-making and engagement in risky behaviors as the adolescent grapples with defining their identity without the firm, positive foundation provided by a father. On the other hand, certain children may react to the absence of a father by cultivating increased autonomy and self-sufficiency. Although these attributes can hold positive aspects, the expectation of being self-reliant from a young age can induce stress and precipitate premature maturation. As a result, adolescents may skip essential developmental stages, potentially impairing the formation of a well-rounded and balanced identity.

The significance of a father's role in adolescent identity development cannot be overstated. Fathers play a multifaceted role in shaping their children's lives and establishing the groundwork for their foundation. They contribute to bolstering their confidence, instilling moral values, and enhancing their capacity to navigate life's adversities.

Gender Identity and Father-Child Relationships:

As adolescents stand at the important junction of life, gender identity development emerges as an important aspect of overall identity formation in children, significantly influenced by the father-child dynamic. Fathers can profoundly impact their children's understanding and expression of gender through their attitudes, behaviors, and interactions.

In many instances, fathers serve as one of the primary role models for children as they begin to comprehend gender roles and behaviors. The manner in which a father demonstrates his masculinity, free from the constraints of stoicism, his interactions with others, and his fulfillment of familial and societal roles all play a significant role in shaping the child's early perceptions of gender. For example, a father who actively engages in household chores and caregiving tasks presents a multifaceted, adaptable model of masculinity that transcends conventional norms. Witnessing their father embody such qualities promotes a more inclusive perspective on gender roles, fostering a belief in equality and collaboration that children can then incorporate into their future relationships.

For the cultivation of these qualities in the children, fathers who encourage their children to explore a range of interests, regardless of traditional gender norms, contribute to a more open exploration of gender identity. This encouragement can include supporting sons in emotional expression often reserved for daughters or motivating daughters to pursue interests traditionally seen as masculine, like certain sports or sciences. Such support helps children develop confidence in their interests and abilities, irrespective of societal gender expectations, promoting a well-rounded sense of self.

The emotional involvement of a father is a core part of the development of a child's understanding of gender identity. When fathers are emotionally available, they provide a secure environment for children to express their feelings and doubts about their gender identity without fear of judgment or rejection. This support is essential for children, particularly during adolescence, as they navigate the complex feelings associated with their emerging gender identity. Looking back at the historical aspect of fatherhood, we often see a depiction of strictness and imposition of unnecessary rules by fathers onto their children, reflecting a lack of comprehension regarding concepts such as emotional engagement in this role. For instance, daughters frequently experienced the rigidity stemming from their fathers' stoic masculinity.

Fathers who openly challenge gender stereotypes provide a critical counter-narrative that helps children learn to value individuality over conformity. By challenging traditional gender roles and presenting alternative ways of being, fathers help their children develop a more flexible and individualized understanding of gender. This could entail a father sharing his own encounters with societal gender expectations or pointing out instances from media and society where gender norms are challenged and redefined.

While a father's impact on gender identity can be significantly beneficial, his absence can create a noticeable vacuum. Without a father figure, children may miss out on a male role model who can demonstrate the spectrum of masculinity or provide support in challenging gender norms. This absence can sometimes lead to uncertainty or confusion about gender roles, especially for boys who may be seeking models of what it means to be a man. Families and communities may have to seek out alternative role models who can offer well-rounded, positive demonstrations of gender expression.

Children without a male paternal figure may often seek other males who can serve as role models. This search can lead them to connect with uncles, coaches, teachers, or family friends who can offer guidance, support, and a model of masculinity that encourages positive development. These figures play a vital role in helping children form a secure and balanced gender identity. In many cases, the broader community and extended family members can step in to fill the void left by an absent father.

This group can include women who model strength and resilience, providing examples that blur traditional gender distinctions. Community programs and schools also play a significant role, offering resources and mentorship programs that support children in exploring and affirming their gender identity in a father's absence. Overall, the influence of a father's role in the development of gender identity in children is vast and deeply influential. Fathers who engage positively and openly in this aspect of their child's development can foster a more inclusive, confident, and secure sense of gender identity, equipping children to navigate the complexities of gender with confidence and self-assurance.

Psychological Impact of Paternal Absence:

The absence of a father can have a profound psychological impact on a child's development. If a father figure is absent from children's lives, it often leaves an emotional rift in their lives. This rift or void can manifest as attachment issues, where children may struggle to form secure relationships. They may run the risk of either becoming overly clingy and dependent in their relationships or displaying an avoidant attachment style, distancing themselves to avoid potential rejection or loss. These patterns often stem from the fundamental insecurity that develops when a primary caregiver is absent, affecting the children's ability to trust and connect with others.

Children who lack a father figure often grapple with lower self-esteem. They may wrestle with feelings of inherent unworthiness or abandonment, questioning why their father is absent. This can result in a fragile sense of self and identity ambiguity, as the child lacks a clear, supportive paternal figure to assist them in navigating the complexities of growing up and understanding their identity. This is especially pronounced for male children who lack a male role model at home.

The absence of a father is statistically linked to a higher risk of behavioral problems in children (Kim & Glassgow, 2018). Without the disciplinary and guiding influence of a father, children might act out as a cry for attention or as a means of expressing unresolved anger and sadness. Such behaviors may manifest as aggression, defiance of rules, or involvement in risky activities during adolescence, potentially leading them into encounters with the criminal justice system or mental health institutions. The absence of a father figure often results in fewer boundaries and consequences being enforced, which are essential elements in teaching children about appropriate behavior and self-discipline.

Psychologically, the absence of a father also impacts a child's cognitive development and academic performance. Fathers often provide unique cognitive stimulation and support that is different from maternal interactions. They might encourage risk-taking and competition, promote problem-solving, and motivate academic achievement. Without this influence, children may lack the necessary encouragement and drive to reach their fullest potential, leading to underperformance in educational settings.

Amid increasing controversies and a manipulative environment, the presence of a father figure has become more crucial than ever. Illustrating the profound impact of a father's presence or absence during a child's adolescent years, the role of fatherhood emerges as irreplaceable, emphasizing the significance of its influence within the household. This role shapes the future of society, as fathers impart crucial moral values to their children, guiding them to navigate the world with dignity and respect. Essentially, fathers play a transformative and uplifting role in shaping the generations to come through their teachings and guidance.

"When you teach your son, you teach your son's son."

~ The Talmud

Chapter 5: Educational Achievement

A child's mental journey begins in the cradle of innocence, surrounded by the warmth of family. In this nurturing environment of constant learning and observation, the child takes their first steps, building the foundation for the challenges they will face in life.

During this period, a child's enthusiasm for learning and quest for knowledge is nurtured through the active engagement of parents, particularly fathers. A father who embodies the essence of fatherhood comprehends the vital role he plays in fostering his children's growth and development.

A father establishes and nourishes the roots of the child as he indulges them in enriching activities like playing games, puzzles, reading, or even gardening, which enhance the cognitive development of the child. Various studies have revealed that the healthy involvement of a father in a child's life enables them to develop a higher IQ as well as verbal and problem-solving skills (The Ways Fathers Impact Child Development, 2022).

This chapter explores the crevices of educational impact on children's lives and the necessity it carries in the cultivation of a respectable and stable adulthood. Venturing further, it will shed light on the influence of a father—a pivotal role that brightens the often-overlooked aspects of guiding responsibly. The chapter will then explore the crucial need for a father's involvement in nurturing these qualities in their children's lives.

Children's mental development, although a lifetime journey, is segregated into different phases, the very first being the time before joining primary school. In this phase, the role of a father's involvement curates the child's mindset into a progressive and goal-oriented one. Before delving into the role of a father, let's first examine its necessity—the urgent need to understand how and why educational achievements play a crucial role in children's lives.

Impact of Educational Achievements on Children:

Knowledge is the master key, unlocking the secrets and deep essence of life. The pursuit and affirmation of knowledge cultivate confidence and foster self-respect in people of all ages, especially in children. Educational success is not merely a gateway to better job prospects; it is a cornerstone that supports a child's development into a well-rounded and confident individual.

Education goes beyond imparting facts to a child; it unlocks doors to new worlds, both literally and metaphorically. The journey through learning empowers children, boosting their self-esteem as they master new skills and conquer academic challenges. Educational achievement extends far beyond the confines of traditional academic success, weaving its way into the core of a child's development.

As children analyze and walk through the complexities of school, from deciphering the basics of arithmetic to analyzing the motifs of classic literature, they are doing much more than just accumulating knowledge—they are laying the foundation for a future filled with possibilities. Success in school translates into a sense of competence and efficacy, brick by brick, in building their mindset. Every quiz aced, and every project completed to satisfaction doesn't just boost grades but also elevates a child's self-image. As they start recognizing their own capabilities and intellect, this perception influences their eagerness to embrace fresh challenges and their ability to persevere through difficulties.

This growing self-confidence is a crucial byproduct of educational achievement, empowering children to set ambitious goals and strive to achieve them.

As one delves further into the roots of this topic, the sight emerges, visualizing the aspect that academic achievement nurtures critical life skills that are indispensable in adulthood. Effective communication, for instance, is honed through myriad classroom discussions and written assignments, enabling children to express their thoughts and ideas clearly and persuasively.

Problem-solving skills are sharpened each time they tackle complex mathematical equations or scientific experiments, teaching them to think logically and creatively. These skills, cultivated on the fertile ground of education, are vital for personal and professional success later in life. Furthermore, thriving academically can significantly enhance a child's social standing among peers, which in turn can affect their social skills development.

Achievements in school often lead to positive recognition from teachers and classmates, which can improve a child's social interactions and acceptance. This aids in the curating of better relationships and a more supportive peer environment, reinforcing the child's academic efforts and emotional well-being. The worldview of children is also shaped as they see their hard work being manifested into success—the result of their efforts and mental capability.

Adolescence marks a stage in life when the human mindset is at its peak receptivity, absorbing knowledge with a heightened susceptibility. As previously discussed, the process of learning begins in childhood through the art of observation. During this phase, the curiosity to explore knowledge across various fields captivates the mind. As children explore different subjects, they learn about diverse cultures, historical events, and global issues, broadening their perspectives and fostering a deeper understanding of the world around them, cladding their identity with the shield of knowledge.

This expanded perspective fosters empathy, tolerance, and a sense of global citizenship, qualities that are increasingly essential in today's society.

Influence on Academic Success:

Complementing the previous point, nurturing the ability for such achievements in the child to progress in the educational realm, a father's role structures the core for such capabilities in the children. The narrative of a father's influence on a child's academic success is compelling and rich with potential. Fathers, through their actions and attitudes toward education, become the building blocks in shaping their children's academic outlook and performance.

This influence stretches from the early years of schooling through to higher education, marking a critical component in a child's educational journey. Active involvement of fathers in homework and school-related activities significantly enhances a child's educational experience. This involvement shows children that their educational endeavors are worthwhile and deserving of time and effort. When a father sits down to help with a math problem or discusses the content of a history lesson, it not only aids in comprehension but also demonstrates practical support.

This shared academic activity helps to normalize education as a regular part of family life, instilling a habit of learning and curiosity. Fathers who express a positive attitude toward education and its benefits convey to their children the importance of academic pursuits. They become role models not just in their behaviors but through the values they instill.

Children who see their fathers valuing education are more likely to develop similar attitudes, which can lead to higher levels of educational achievement. This example also includes demonstrating perseverance—fathers who approach challenges with a positive mindset teach their children to face academic pressures with resilience.

Moreover, fathers who set expectations for academic success tend to raise children who aim to meet or exceed those expectations. These expectations can motivate children to strive for higher performance, particularly when paired with supportive guidance rather than pressure. The balance of expectation and support can foster an environment where children feel empowered to achieve their best. Fatherly support in education extends beyond academic learning. It also includes emotional support during school-related challenges. Fathers who are accessible and responsive to their children's academic stress can help them manage anxieties related to school.

This emotional backing is crucial during exams, school transitions, and other stressful academic periods, providing a safety net that reassures children that they are not alone in their educational journey. The role of a father in academic success is, therefore, multifaceted, impacting not only the cognitive aspects of education but also the emotional and motivational dimensions. Fathers who actively engage in their child's education can make a profound difference in their child's academic trajectory, contributing significantly to their overall success and enthusiasm for learning.

A true father figure anchors a child's life by making them aware of and knowledgeable about the negative influences present in society, particularly in schools. They provide guidance and shape their mindset, steering them away from the point where they might begin to condone the actions of violent groups or peers who undermine the value of education. In essence, fathers can help navigate their children's lives during periods of hostilities and negativity found in schools, such as bullying, drugs, and violence.

Research shows that children with actively involved fathers are twice as enthusiastic about their study goals and motivation to attend college, and they are 80% less likely to end up in jail due to the supportive presence of a father (Importance of Fathers & Statistics, n.d.).

The significance of fatherly involvement in education is immense, shaping not only academic outcomes but also the holistic development of children. Fathers who are deeply engaged in their children's educational processes provide a supportive framework that goes beyond academic assistance, nurturing an environment ripe for personal and intellectual growth. One of the most direct impacts of fatherly involvement is seen in the consistent encouragement and support fathers can provide.

Involvement in education also allows fathers to be in tune with the educational needs and challenges their children face. This close observation helps fathers tailor their support according to their children's unique learning styles and academic requirements. For instance, a father might notice a child struggling with reading. He could introduce books that align with the child's interests, thereby nurturing a love for reading while also improving literacy skills.

The supportive presence of a positive father figure helps children develop respect for structured learning environments, leading to improved classroom behavior and social interactions— qualities they can carry into adulthood. Fatherly involvement is often overlooked and reduced to the role of a breadwinner when, in reality, it plays a vital role in shaping children's future educational aspirations.

Fathers who discuss future academic and career goals offer a vision that guides their children's ambitions. By sharing their own life journey, highlighting the challenges they overcame, and recounting stories of other accomplished and driven individuals, they inspire and shape their children's objectives. This information is crucial as it helps children visualize their future and understand the steps needed to achieve their goals, instilling a sense of purpose and direction in their academic endeavors.

As the chapter draws to a close, a vision emerges of fatherhood as a fundamental component in shaping a child's existence. The genuine fulfillment of this role guides children along a path enriched with knowledge, respect, and responsibility, serving as their guide and ensuring the future generation inherits these invaluable traits.

"Intelligence plus character—that is the goal of true education."

~ Martin Luther King Jr.

Chapter 6: Emotional Well-being

From an early age, children encounter many fears that can burden them and potentially hinder the development of their full potential. Childhood, a vulnerable phase marked by dependence, is shaped by the decisions of their elders. Johannes Giesinger emphasizes this vulnerability, noting that children are often unable to avoid threats or dangers (Bagattini, 2019).

There are a myriad of reasons, instances, and situations that inflict mental and emotional pressure upon children. For example, within the school system, which is supposed to be a nurturing environment, schools can become battlegrounds where students face bullying and intimidation from both peers and teachers. Surrounded by such an environment with no outlet for their feelings, children can become burdened with emotions like frustration, anger, and loneliness. Each of these emotions can erode their desire to attend school, leading to depression. Their emotional state can deteriorate, and their natural abilities become suppressed under the weight of unaddressed trauma.

This inability to express their depression and struggles often occurs in children raised in homes lacking emotional support, where they fear being blamed for their challenges and fears. Without any hope in sight, they tend to face their difficulties with fear and hopelessness.

Many, falling victim to the claws of loneliness created by these hardships, confine themselves in a prison of helplessness, diminishing their decision-making ability. Eventually, this long and arduous struggle can steer them onto a narrow path, potentially jeopardizing their future. However, when genuine fatherhood is introduced into the equation, it becomes a sanctuary for children—a comforting presence where they can release their accumulated stress and burdens. This support and hope provide the strength and motivation they need to navigate life's challenges and pursue their dreams with optimism.

This chapter narrates the trials and tribulations children face in the emotional realm and illuminates the role of fatherhood as the ray of hope in such moments. Delving deeper into the depths of this concept, this topic is polished by understanding both perspectives and how fathers can navigate through this maze.

Emotional Support Systems:

Fatherhood encompasses many facets, each impacting family and societal evolution. One crucial branch of it extends its shade toward the emotional nurturing of children. As the concept of fatherhood evolved over the ages, people began to understand its essentiality in children's lives. **A good father cultivates and nurtures an atmosphere in the home where the children feel comfortable revealing their burdens.** This requires fostering open communication. By sharing his own struggles, a father encourages similar behavior in his children. He understands that he is a role model, and his actions hold significant weight in the eyes of the children.

In many households, fathers sometimes fear appearing weak and tend to internalize their troubles, which can create a tense home environment. Witnessing this, children learn to suppress their own emotions, perpetuating the cycle.

Yet, when a father embodies the essence of genuine fatherhood, he can serve as a steadfast source of emotional support through attentive listening. Children naturally gravitate toward dependable figures who care for them and attend to their needs. Unfortunately, when they encounter disinterest or dismissive reactions, their trust wears away. With each instance, the bond weakens, and children come to view their parents as individuals to evade, fearing additional disappointment or anger.

Nevertheless, a father who perceives his child's seemingly trivial challenges as weighty burdens will listen intently and provide invaluable guidance. A true champion of fatherhood explains the complexities of challenges faced by children, fostering the understanding that life is not linear but a path with unexpected turns and trials.

By revealing his own hardships, explaining the world's complexities, and embedding wisdom within his advice or stories, a father prepares his children for moments of despair. He teaches them flexibility and acceptance that things may not always go as planned, equipping them to navigate challenges with maturity and reason. From the very beginning, a father nurtures and nourishes their emotional intelligence, guiding them on a path for further growth.

Handling Emotions and Stress:

Fathers often face a dilemma when their child confesses to wrongdoing. The decision on how to respond can leave them conflicted, torn between the extremes of harsh punishment and unconditional leniency—each carrying the risk of negatively impacting the child's future.

Harsh punishment can drive children into depression, while unconditional reassurance may lead them to repeat the offense, fostering a sense of impunity. Many cases have highlighted where fathers, fully aware of the severity of their children's wrongdoings, choose to reassure them and cover up their actions. On the other hand, we also see the tragic outcomes of children resorting to suicide or running away from home to escape abuse. When discipline is mishandled, it can become more harmful than helpful, acting as a poison rather than a cure.

In these situations, a father's role as a thoughtful disciplinarian becomes essential in keeping the child's life on track. Since children rely on their elders for guidance, a father creates a path with rational rules and guidelines to help the child navigate life. When a child falters, a good father understands the importance of controlled anger and uses appropriate discipline. He carefully untangles the child's mind from the web of stressful events, gently steering them in the right direction. However, if the child is left to handle these challenges alone, unaddressed emotions can build up, ultimately undermining their confidence and future prospects.

Therefore, fathers must adopt parenting techniques (that will be discussed in the latter part of the book) that shield children from such suffering and equip them with the wisdom to navigate difficult situations.

Growing up with clear rules, a supportive environment, and proper discipline techniques fosters confidence and an optimistic outlook in the children. Such an approach, while beneficial throughout childhood, becomes vital during adolescence.

Adolescents face the burden of academic pressures, peer relationships, self-discovery, and puberty, where their emotional state remains more vulnerable to the shadows of depression. A father's strategic involvement, guiding them with his wisdom and subtly supporting them in the right direction, can alleviate some of this pressure, allowing them to focus on achieving their goals.

Impact of Paternal Involvement on Mental Health:

Today's adolescents and children face significant stress from family conflicts, academic pressure, and peer relationships. Adding to the mental burden, social media, showcasing curated success stories, creates a void of insecurity as children become fixated on their social standing. Exposure to a myriad of stressors takes a toll on their mental health. According to the APA's Stress in America poll (Bethune, 2014), adolescents report higher stress levels than adults (5.8 vs. 3.9 on a 10-point scale).

Under the shadow of depression, their goals dim with stress obstructing their vision, leading to isolation and a decline in overall functionality. Their ability to make sound decisions weakens as the darkness of depression deepens. In these moments, parents, armed with wisdom and experience, should be vigilant in recognizing subtle changes in their children's behavior.

While parents cannot cure mental health issues, they should understand when professional help is necessary. Unfortunately, some dismiss mental health concerns, hoping time will heal or fearing societal judgment. A true parent recognizes that emotional and mental challenges can become barriers, hindering a child's dreams and aspirations. Seeking professional help can truly be life-saving, freeing a child from the grip of despair.

Sometimes, children may mimic their parents' emotional and mental struggles, leading parents to believe such behavior is normal. In these cases, mentors or other figures in society become a lifeline for the child. However, parents must understand that seeking mental health support is not a source of shame but an act of love and empathy – love that can save their child from a lifetime of suffering.

Building Bridges, Not Walls:

The landscape of fatherhood has undergone a significant transformation. Today, a father is a confidante, a cheerleader, and a role model who actively participates in his children's lives. This shift reflects the growing understanding of a child's emotional needs and the crucial role fathers play in nurturing them.

Strong father-child relationships foster a sense of security and self-worth in children. Children with involved fathers demonstrate higher academic achievement, better social skills, and a reduced risk of engaging in risky behaviors (Lamb, Pleck, Lerner & Steinberg, 2002). Fathers who prioritize these relationships not only contribute to their children's well-being but also enrich their own lives. The joy, love, and sense of accomplishment that comes from witnessing a child's growth and development is unparalleled.

Nonetheless, the path of fatherhood is not without its challenges. Single fathers, stepfathers, and fathers who work long hours encounter unique challenges in forming strong connections with their children. One of my associates, James, is currently navigating through this rough patch of being a stepfather to a child. James is in a common-law marriage, and both he and his partner have one child each from previous relationships. James confided in me about the challenges he faces, particularly with his partner's 12-year-old child, who struggles to respect him because he is not their biological father. At times, the child would dismiss James, saying, "I don't have to listen to you because you are not my father."

Despite these hurdles, dedication and a commitment to quality time can help to bridge the gap. Even after anticipating these difficulties when entering the relationship, James remains determined not to give up. He continues to make efforts to connect with the young man and improve their relationship. He is actively collaborating with his partner to navigate and resolve the situation. James concluded, "It's difficult, but I can't quit."

Ultimately, fatherhood is a journey of constant learning and self-discovery. There is no single "right" way to be a father, but there is a right approach — an approach built on love, communication, and a willingness to be present in a child's life. Fathers who embrace this approach become guiding lights, illuminating their children's paths and empowering them to navigate the complexities of life with courage, resilience, and a hopeful heart.

Building Emotional Resilience:

As children navigate the ups and downs of life, emotional resilience becomes a cornerstone of their overall well-being.

Fathers play a critical role in fostering this resilience, equipping their children with the tools they need to withstand adversity and bounce back from setbacks. Emotional resilience is not an inherent trait but a learned skill developed through supportive relationships and positive role modeling. A father who openly addresses his own challenges and demonstrates effective coping mechanisms sets a powerful example for his children.

By showing that it is normal to encounter difficulties and that these can be overcome with patience and perseverance, he instills a sense of strength and confidence in his children. This modeling is particularly important during adolescence when children are more likely to face significant emotional and social pressures. In addition to modeling resilience, fathers can actively teach their children strategies to manage stress and regulate their emotions. Techniques such as mindfulness, deep breathing exercises, and reflective journaling can be introduced and practiced together. By engaging in these activities, fathers not only provide their children with practical tools but also create opportunities for bonding and open communication.

Fathers also have a vital role in assisting children to see negative experiences in a different light. By guiding their children to see challenges as opportunities for growth rather than insurmountable obstacles, fathers help them develop a growth mindset. This shift in perspective encourages children to embrace failures as learning experiences and to persist in the face of difficulty. Furthermore, fathers can support their children's emotional resilience by fostering a strong sense of self-efficacy.

When children believe in their ability to influence their own lives and outcomes, they are more likely to take proactive steps in challenging situations. Fathers can nurture this belief by providing opportunities for their children to make decisions, solve problems, and take on responsibilities within the family.

Nurturing Emotional Intelligence:

Emotional intelligence is another critical area in which fathers can make a significant impact. Emotional intelligence involves the ability to recognize, understand, and manage one's own emotions, as well as to empathize with the emotions of others. High emotional intelligence is linked to better mental health, stronger relationships, and greater success in both personal and professional life.

Fathers can nurture emotional intelligence in their children by creating an environment where emotions are acknowledged and valued. This begins with validating their children's feelings, whether positive or negative, and helping them articulate those emotions. For instance, when a child feels angry or upset, a father can help them identify the emotion and discuss its underlying causes. This process not only helps children feel understood but also teaches them to process and express their emotions in healthy ways.

In addition to emotional validation, fathers can teach empathy by encouraging their children to consider other people's perspectives. This can be done through discussions about social situations, storytelling, or role-playing exercises. By fostering empathy, fathers can help their children build stronger interpersonal relationships and develop a deeper understanding of the world around them.

Creating a Balanced Approach to Discipline:

Fathers play a crucial role in shaping their children's emotional well-being through effective discipline. By combining clear expectations and consequences with support and understanding, fathers can foster self-discipline and accountability in their children. This balanced approach ensures that children learn responsibility without feeling overwhelmed or unloved. Fathers can create a balanced discipline strategy by involving their children in the process of setting rules and consequences.

This collaborative approach makes children more likely to follow the rules and helps them understand the reasons behind them. When consequences are necessary, they should be applied consistently and fairly, with a focus on teaching rather than punishing. In situations where a child has made a mistake, a father can use the opportunity to discuss the behavior and its impact, exploring ways to make amends and learn from the experience.

This reflective process encourages children to take responsibility for their actions and to develop a deeper understanding of right and wrong.

Building a Legacy of Love and Support:

The impact of a father's involvement in his child's emotional development extends far beyond childhood. The lessons learned and the support provided during these formative years create a lasting foundation for emotional health and resilience.

Fathers who prioritize their children's emotional well-being leave a legacy of love and support that echoes throughout their children's lives. As fathers strive to build this legacy, it is important to remember that perfection is not the goal. Rather, it is the consistent effort to be present, to listen, and to guide with compassion and wisdom that makes the difference.

Fathers who embrace the journey of emotional nurturing with an open heart, mind, and a willingness to grow alongside their children will find that the rewards are immeasurable. In conclusion, fatherhood is a profound and multifaceted role that encompasses far more than traditional notions of provision and discipline. It is a dynamic journey that involves nurturing emotional well-being, fostering resilience, and building strong, supportive relationships. Through love, communication, and active involvement, fathers have the power to shape their children's futures, guiding them toward a life of emotional health, fulfillment, and success.

Remember, the greatest legacy a father can leave his children is not wealth or power but the indelible imprint of his love, guidance, and unwavering belief in their potential.

"Real fatherhood means love and commitment and sacrifice and a willingness to share responsibility and not walking away from one's children."

~ William Bennett

Chapter 7: Communication and Bonding

Communication has always been the core of human relationships since the beginning of time.

This concept hinges on grasping the nuances of conversational etiquette and assessing the other party's sophistication to shape the dialogue accordingly. Examining historical conflicts underscores the critical role of communication—it can either sow chaos or foster peace.

Likewise, this fundamental aspect of human life is crucial in family dynamics, helping children develop a foundational understanding of how to navigate the world. Based on the nature of communication, healthy or negative, the lives of the children are steered by their parents. The data regarding depression and anxiety in U.S. children of 3 to 17 years old reveals that 4.4% (approximately 2.7 million) are victims of depression, and 9.4% (approximately 5.8 million) suffer from anxiety (Centers for Disease Control and Prevention, 2023).

While on the other side of the spectrum, we see children who are not victims of such diseases. Why is that?

This can stem from their positive communication dynamic with their parents. Challenges arise for children when they lack a safe space to express their anger and frustration while navigating early life hurdles. Without a reliable support system, like understanding parents, they may fear confiding in them due to potential negative reactions or dismissive responses.

These cases are more common among single-parent households where the parent, whether father or mother, is busy with earning and providing the children with their basic needs. Amidst this juggling of responsibilities, they end up sacrificing the most important aspect of love a parent can bless their children with – communicating and being there for them. Parenting, especially for single fathers, is a journey laced with trials and victories, and healthy communication between them and the kid remains the biggest hurdle in this path.

Successfully navigating this obstacle can greatly enhance a child's development and establish a lasting, strong bond of expression. Conversely, failure to do so can erode trust and the parent-child relationship, potentially impacting the child's mental well-being.

Fatherhood, a role as rewarding as it is challenging, is significantly influenced by the quality of communication between a father and his children. Developing effective communication is not merely about exchanging words; it encompasses listening, understanding, and responding in a manner that nurtures trust and fosters deep connections. In this chapter, we will explore the intricacies of effective communication, the role it plays in building trust and understanding, and how it nurtures positive father-child relationships.

Developing Effective Communication:

Effective communication is vital to any healthy relationship, and fatherhood is no exception. For fathers, this means more than just giving advice or issuing commands. It involves active listening, empathetic responses, and creating an environment where children feel heard and valued. Cultivation of effective communication involves multiple facets that contribute to the nurturing of this element in the relationship between a father and a child.

Active Listening:

Active listening is more than just hearing words; it is about fully engaging with what the child is saying. This means giving undivided attention, maintaining eye contact, and responding with verbal and non-verbal cues that show you are listening. Nodding, using affirmative sounds like "I see" or "That's interesting," and asking follow-up questions demonstrate that you are genuinely interested in what the child is sharing.

Active listening also involves acknowledging the child's feelings and validating their experiences. For example, if a child is upset about a conflict with a friend, a father might say, "I can see that you're really hurt by what happened. That must have been really tough." This kind of response shows empathy and helps the child feel understood. The child perceives the emotional presence of their father, and the threads of trust start to knit between them.

Creating an Open Environment:

Creating an open environment where children feel safe to express their thoughts and emotions is crucial. This can be achieved by setting aside regular, distraction-free time for conversations. Whether it's during dinner, a walk, or before bedtime, having consistent opportunities for open dialogue helps establish a routine where children know they have a safe space to talk.

In an open environment, it is also important to avoid negative reactions such as dismissiveness, criticism, or anger, as observed in most households where firm and strict ways are presumed to be an effective element in the upbringing of children. When children fear negative responses, they are less likely to share their true feelings and thoughts and keep those emotions buried inside. Eventually, these emotions haunt their mental capabilities and could drive them into a state of depression. Instead, fathers must strive to respond with patience, support, and understanding, even when the conversation is difficult.

Positive Language and Reinforcement:

Using positive language and reinforcement plays a significant role in effective communication. Instead of focusing on what the child did wrong, fathers should highlight what the child did right and encourage positive behaviors. For instance, instead of saying, "Don't be so lazy," a father might say, "I really appreciate it when you help out with chores. It shows responsibility." This statement encourages the child to be more responsible, while the first response would drive them toward stubbornness, nurturing within them hesitation whenever they are around their father.

Positive reinforcement can also be used to build self-esteem and motivate children. Praise and recognition for efforts and achievements, no matter how small, can boost a child's confidence and encourage them to continue striving. For example, acknowledging a child's hard work on a school project with specific praise like, "You put a lot of effort into this project, and it shows in the details," reinforces their effort and dedication instead of discarding their efforts with remarks like "You could have done better."

Non-Verbal Communication:

Non-verbal communication is equally important in conveying messages and emotions. Facial expressions, body language, and tone of voice can all impact how a message is received. For example, a warm smile and gentle tone can make a child feel loved and secure, while crossed arms and a stern voice can create a sense of fear or anxiety. Fathers can benefit from being mindful of their non-verbal cues, ensuring they align with their verbal messages. Consistency between what is said and how it is said helps build trust and clarity in communication.

Encouraging Open-ended Questions:

Asking open-ended questions encourages children to think more deeply and express themselves more fully. Instead of asking questions that can be answered with a simple yes or no, fathers need to ask questions that require more elaborate responses. For example, asking, "What was the best part of your day?" instead of "Did you have a good day?" invites the child to share more about their experiences and feelings. Open-ended questions also help children develop critical thinking and communication skills. They learn to articulate their thoughts and feelings more clearly and gain confidence in expressing themselves.

Being a Role Model:

Fathers play a crucial role as role models in communication. Children often emulate the behavior they observe in their parents. By demonstrating effective communication skills, such as listening actively, expressing feelings openly and respectfully, and resolving conflicts calmly, fathers set a powerful example for their children to follow.

Being a role model also involves admitting mistakes and showing a willingness to learn and grow. When fathers acknowledge their own communication shortcomings and make efforts to improve, they teach their children the importance of continuous self-improvement and humility.

Developing effective communication is an ongoing process that requires intentional effort and practice. By engaging in active listening, creating an open environment, using positive language, being mindful of non-verbal cues, encouraging open-ended questions, and serving as a role model, fathers hold the key to fostering a deep and meaningful connection with their children.

This connection lays the foundation for building trust and understanding, which are essential for nurturing positive father-child relationships. As we explore fatherhood, let us remember that the quality of our relationships with our children is profoundly influenced by how well we communicate, understand, and connect with them.

Building Trust and Understanding:

Trust is the foundation of any strong relationship, and building it requires consistency, reliability, and empathy. Understanding, on the other hand, involves truly grasping the child's perspective and validating their feelings. Both trust and understanding are critical components of a healthy father-child relationship and are closely linked to effective communication. The following aspects aid in building trust and understanding between a father and a child:

Consistency and Reliability:

Trust is built over time through consistent and reliable behavior. When fathers keep their promises and follow through on their commitments, they demonstrate to their children that they are dependable.

This reliability helps children feel secure and reinforces their trust in their fathers. For instance, if a father promises to attend a child's school event, making sure to be there as promised sends a powerful message about reliability and commitment. Consistency also involves maintaining a stable and predictable environment. Children thrive on routine and knowing what to expect from their parents.

Consistent rules, expectations, and responses help create a sense of security. For example, having regular family meals where everyone shares stories about their day can establish a comforting routine that fosters open communication.

Honesty and Transparency:

Honesty is the knot that fastens the bond of trust. Fathers should strive to be truthful with their children, even when the truth is difficult. This doesn't mean overwhelming children with adult problems, but it does mean being honest about situations that affect them. For example, if a family is facing financial difficulties, it might be appropriate to explain in simple terms that some adjustments are necessary rather than keeping the child in the dark.

Transparency also involves sharing feelings and thoughts with children in an age-appropriate manner. When fathers are open about their own experiences and emotions, it encourages children to do the same. This kind of openness helps demystify emotions and promotes a culture of honesty within the family.

Empathy and Validation:

Understanding a child's perspective requires empathy – the ability to put oneself in their shoes and see the world through their eyes. Empathetic responses involve acknowledging and validating a child's feelings, even if they seem trivial or irrational from an adult's perspective.

For instance, if a child is upset about losing a game, a father might say, "I can see you're really disappointed about the game. It's okay to feel that way." Validation doesn't necessarily mean agreeing with everything the child says or does; it means recognizing their emotions as real and important.

This validation helps children feel understood and valued, which strengthens their trust in their father. Consider a scenario where a teenager feels overwhelmed by school pressures. Recognizing and validating this stress instead of brushing it off as trivial can have a profound impact.

Building Emotional Safety:

Creating an environment of emotional safety is essential for fostering trust and understanding. Children need to feel that they can express their true feelings without fear of criticism or punishment. Fathers can build this safety by responding to their children's emotions with patience and support. For instance, if a child is angry, instead of reacting with anger in return, a father might calmly say, "I can see you're really upset. Let's talk about what's bothering you."

Emotional safety also involves setting boundaries and enforcing rules in a fair and respectful manner. When children know what is expected of them and understand the consequences of their actions, they feel more secure. Fair discipline that focuses on teaching rather than punishing helps children learn from their mistakes while maintaining trust in their father's fairness and support.

Active Engagement and Interest:

Actively engaging in a child's life and showing genuine interest in their activities, thoughts, and feelings is a powerful way to build trust and understanding. Fathers can promote this engagement by participating in their children's hobbies, attending their events, and having regular, meaningful conversations. A father who helps his child with a science project or attends a basketball game demonstrates a deep investment in their child's life. Active engagement also involves asking open-ended questions that encourage children to share more about their experiences and thoughts.

Handling Conflicts with Care:

Conflicts are inevitable in any relationship, but how they are handled can either build or erode trust. Fathers, as role models, should approach conflicts with a calm and constructive attitude, focusing on resolving the issue rather than assigning blame. Listening to the child's perspective, acknowledging their feelings, and finding mutually acceptable solutions helps maintain trust and reinforces understanding.

For example, if a conflict arises over curfew times, a father might listen to the child's reasons for wanting a later curfew, explain his own concerns, and then negotiate a compromise. This approach shows respect for the child's viewpoint and demonstrates a willingness to understand and work together toward a solution.

Building trust and understanding requires consistent effort and empathy. By hosting these qualities in their parenting, fathers can develop deep and lasting trust and understanding. These elements are essential for nurturing positive father-child relationships, providing a solid foundation for effective communication and bonding. As we explore the concept of fatherhood, let us remember that trust and understanding are not given but earned through our actions and interactions with our children.

Positive Father-Child Relationships:

A positive father-child relationship is characterized by love, respect, and mutual support. Such relationships are nurtured through consistent efforts to communicate effectively and build trust and understanding.

Fathers who prioritize these aspects are better equipped to guide their children through the complexities of life, providing a stable and supportive presence. Fathers need to be actively engaged in their children's lives to build and nurture a positive relationship. But most importantly, creating a positive home environment is essential for fostering this type of relationship. An environment where children don't feel tense about sharing or revealing their burdens and experiences, a house where the factor of fear is eliminated from children's lives and replaced with an open and affectionate environment where there is no judgment but guiding them with respect and love in the right direction.

This involvement goes beyond providing for their physical needs; it includes participating in their education, hobbies, and social activities. Being present at important events, showing interest in their daily lives, and celebrating their achievements, no matter how small, reinforces the bond between father and child.

Another crucial aspect is showing affection and appreciation. Simple gestures like hugs, words of praise, and expressions of love contribute significantly to a child's emotional well-being. These gestures can help build a sense of feeling respected and being seen by their role model, the person they look up to. These actions convey to the child that they are valued and loved unconditionally, which in turn nourishes a positive self-image and confidence.

According to World-Metrics research, children who have a strong early relationship with their fathers are less likely to become distressed and cry when they are in new or unfamiliar surroundings (Father Involvement Statistics • WorldMetrics, 2024). This underscores the importance of effective communication and the need to build a trusting relationship with children from the moment they are born.

Communication and bonding are the soul of the role of fatherhood. Developing effective communication lays the groundwork for building trust and understanding, which are essential for nurturing positive father-child relationships. Fathers who master these elements create a supportive and loving environment where their children can thrive emotionally, socially, and intellectually and are liberated from the prison of depression and self-loathing.

"Children need models rather than critics."

~ Joseph Joubert

Chapter 8: Active Involvement in Parenting

Over the centuries, the role of fatherhood has evolved significantly, gaining more depth and complexity. One key aspect of this evolution is active involvement in parenting, which is essential for the development and well-being of children.

In a world where the demands of work and personal responsibilities often compete for attention, the role of an engaged father becomes even more critical. The birth of a child profoundly changes the course of a parent's life, especially for single parents, who encounter numerous challenges simply to remain involved in their child's life.

For example, military service creates challenging work and family dynamics. For single parents, this often leads to feelings of depression as they struggle to balance job responsibilities with being present in their child's life, all while striving to provide the best for their children.

This chapter will delve into the complexities and rewards of being an actively involved parent, exploring the balance between work and personal life, overcoming the challenges of bonding, and finding quality time for meaningful connections with children.

Each of these elements is vital for fathers aiming to be present and engaged in their children's lives, particularly for single parents.

Balancing Work and Personal Life:

One of the most common challenges fathers face is balancing the demands of work with the responsibilities of parenting. As the concept of fatherhood evolved over the centuries, the modern father often juggles multiple roles: the provider, the protector, and the nurturer. This balancing act requires careful time management, setting priorities, and making sacrifices to ensure that both work and family receive the attention they deserve.

Understanding Priorities:

The first step in balancing work and personal life is understanding and setting clear priorities. Fathers need to acknowledge that being actively present and engaged in their children's lives holds equal importance to their career successes. This requires making deliberate choices about how they invest their time and effort.

Making family time a priority doesn't entail disregarding work duties; instead, it involves discovering a sustainable approach to fulfilling both roles proficiently. It is important for fathers to assess their work commitments and identify areas where they can introduce flexibility.

For example, negotiating flexible working hours or remote work options can provide more opportunities to be involved in family activities. Explaining that work can often be demanding. Fathers should also communicate with their employers about the importance of family time and seek support for work-life balance initiatives.

Effective Time Management:

This element is crucial for balancing work and personal responsibilities for a single parent since they are often bound by the complications of providing for their children and being with them. To navigate through such situations, fathers can use various strategies to manage their time better. One effective approach is to create a structured schedule that includes dedicated time for work and family. Using tools like calendars and planners can help fathers visualize their commitments and ensure they allocate time for both professional and personal activities. Setting specific work hours and sticking to them as much as possible helps create a clear boundary between work and home life.

For instance, a father might decide that after 6 PM, all work-related activities are put aside to focus on family. This practice helps in preventing work from encroaching on personal time and vice versa.

Another essential aspect of time management is prioritizing tasks. Fathers could identify the most critical tasks that need immediate attention and focus on completing them first. Delegating tasks, both at work and home, can also help manage the workload more effectively. For example, sharing household chores with a partner or older children can free up time for fathers to engage in more meaningful interactions with their children.

Flexibility and Work-Life Integration:

Modern work environments increasingly offer flexible working arrangements, such as telecommuting, flexible hours, and compressed workweeks. Leveraging these options can significantly help fathers integrate their work and personal lives more seamlessly.

Flexibility allows fathers to be more present for their children without compromising their professional responsibilities. For instance, a father working from home can take short breaks throughout the day to spend time with his children, attend school events, or assist with homework. This flexibility allows for better involvement in children's lives and helps reduce the stress associated with juggling multiple roles.

Work-life integration also involves finding ways to blend work and family activities when appropriate. For example, involving children in work-related tasks that are suitable for their age can provide learning opportunities and foster a sense of inclusion. A father might explain aspects of his job to his children or let them help with simple tasks, making them feel part of his professional life.

Setting Boundaries and Managing Expectations:

Setting clear boundaries between work and personal life is essential for maintaining a healthy balance. Fathers need to communicate their availability and set realistic expectations with both their employers and families. This might involve setting specific times when they are not reachable for work-related matters or establishing family rituals that are strictly adhered to, such as family dinners or weekend outings.

Managing expectations also means being honest about limitations. A father's role includes communicating openly with their family about the demands of their work and explaining when work commitments might interfere with family plans. Similarly, they should discuss the importance of family time with their employers and seek understanding and support for maintaining a work-life balance.

Self-Care and Stress Management:

Balancing work and personal life can be stressful, and fathers need to prioritize self-care to maintain their well-being. According to the Modern Families Index report (The Modern Families Index 2017, n.d.), a third of 2,750 parents surveyed revealed that they regularly feel exhausted and burnt out, and one in five were obligated to work extra hours. Such patterns lead to high-stress levels in fathers, disrupting their connection with their children as they have no energy left to spend time with their children. Taking time for self-care activities, such as exercising, hobbies, or simply relaxing, helps reduce stress and recharge energy levels. A well-rested and healthy father is more capable of being present and engaged with his children.

Stress management techniques, such as exercise, developing a healthy diet, mindfulness, or meditation, can also be beneficial. Fathers should recognize the signs of burnout and take proactive steps to address them. Seeking support from partners, friends, or professionals when needed is crucial for maintaining a healthy balance and being an effective parent.

Finding a balance between work and personal life is a dynamic and ongoing process that requires deliberate effort and planning. By understanding priorities, managing time effectively, leveraging flexibility, setting boundaries, and prioritizing self-care, fathers can create a harmonious balance that allows them to be fully present and engaged in their children's lives. This balance not only benefits the father's well-being but also fosters a nurturing and supportive environment for the entire family.

Overcoming the Challenges of Bonding:

Bonding with children is an essential part of parenting that lays the foundation for a strong and healthy relationship. However, fathers often face various challenges in establishing and maintaining this bond due to time constraints, differing interests, and communication barriers. Overcoming these challenges requires intentional effort, creativity, and a willingness to adapt and grow.

Addressing Time Constraints:

Time constraints are a significant barrier to bonding between fathers and their children. The demands of work, household responsibilities, and other commitments can leave fathers feeling stretched thin, making it difficult to dedicate quality time to their children. To address this issue, fathers must focus on the quality of interactions rather than the quantity.

Prioritizing Quality Time:

Even short periods of dedicated, undistracted time can be meaningful and impactful. Fathers can make a conscious effort to prioritize activities that foster bonding, such as reading together, playing games, or engaging in a shared hobby. For instance, a father might set aside 15 minutes each evening to read a bedtime story or use the time during a commute to have a meaningful conversation with their child. These small, consistent interactions can significantly strengthen the bond between father and child.

Integrating Family Time into Daily Routines:

Integrating family time into daily routines can also help address time constraints. Fathers can involve their children in everyday activities, turning mundane tasks into opportunities for connection. For example, cooking dinner together, working on a household project, or even running errands can become moments of bonding and learning.

Additionally, setting aside specific times for family activities, such as a weekly game night or a regular weekend outing, ensures that time is consistently allocated for family bonding. These routines create a sense of stability and provide regular opportunities for fathers and children to connect.

Finding Common Interests:

Differing interests between fathers and children can pose a challenge to bonding. While fathers and children may have distinct hobbies and preferences, finding common ground is essential for building a strong relationship. To overcome this challenge, fathers can take the initiative to explore new activities together and discover shared interests.

Exploring New Activities Together:

Exploring new activities together allows fathers and children to find common ground and create shared experiences. Fathers can introduce their children to hobbies they enjoy while also showing interest in the child's favorite activities. For example, a father who loves hiking might invite his child on nature walks while also taking the time to learn about the child's interest in video games or music. Conversely, a father who enjoys fishing could involve his children, teaching them the basics while also creating an environment that fosters bonding.

By being open to trying new things and participating in activities outside their comfort zone, fathers can demonstrate their willingness to connect with their children on their terms. This mutual exploration helps build a connection and fosters a sense of partnership and understanding.

Effective Communication:

As discussed in the previous chapter, effective communication is the gateway to a healthy relationship between a parent and a child. Communication barriers can significantly hinder the bonding process. Children, especially teenagers, may be reluctant to open up or share their feelings. Fathers can address this challenge by creating a safe and supportive environment for communication where children feel comfortable expressing themselves.

Creating a Safe Environment:

Creating a safe environment for communication involves establishing trust and showing empathy. Fathers must make it clear that their children can talk to them about anything without fear of judgment or punishment. This requires active listening, validating the child's feelings, and responding with understanding and compassion. For example, if a child comes to their father with a problem, the father should listen attentively, acknowledge the child's emotions, and offer support rather than immediate solutions or criticism. This approach helps build trust and encourages children to share their thoughts and feelings more openly.

Active Listening and Open-Ended Questions:

Active listening is a crucial component of effective communication. Fathers could practice active listening by giving their full attention, making eye contact, and avoiding interruptions when their children speak. This demonstrates that the father values and respects what the child has to say. In the previous chapter, the importance of open-ended questions was highlighted, and asking open-ended questions emerged as a strategy to facilitate deeper conversations.

Addressing Communication Barriers:

Fathers must also be mindful of potential communication barriers and work to address them. For example, cultural differences, generational gaps, or language barriers can affect how fathers and children interact. Being aware of these challenges and making efforts to bridge the gap can improve communication and strengthen the bond. In some cases, seeking external support, such as family therapy or counseling, can be beneficial in addressing communication issues and facilitating healthier interactions. Professional guidance can provide fathers with tools and strategies to improve communication and build stronger relationships with their children.

Overcoming the challenges of bonding requires intentional effort, creativity, and a commitment to understanding and connecting with children. By addressing time constraints, finding common interests, and fostering effective communication, fathers can build strong, meaningful relationships with their children. These efforts not only enhance the father-child bond but also contribute to the overall well-being and development of the child.

Nurturing Meaningful Connection:

In the hustle and bustle of daily life, finding quality time for meaningful connections with children can be a daunting task for fathers. However, this time is crucial for nurturing a strong emotional bond and supporting the child's development. Quality time goes beyond mere presence; it involves engaging in activities that nurture deeper connections, open communication, and shared experiences.

Importance of Quality Time:

Quality time is essential for building a strong father-child relationship. It allows fathers to be actively involved in their children's lives, understand their needs and interests, and provide emotional support. This time together helps children feel valued and loved, boosting their self-esteem and sense of security. As for fathers, these moments create lasting memories and strengthen the familial bond that plays an important role in the development of the children.

Creating Opportunities for Quality Time:

Creating opportunities for quality time requires deliberate planning and effort. Fathers are encouraged to look for everyday moments that can be transformed into meaningful interactions. Here are some strategies to consider:

Integrating Quality Time into Daily Routines:

Daily routines offer numerous opportunities for fathers to connect with their children. Simple activities like having breakfast together, walking the dog, or bedtime routines can become special bonding moments. The key is to be fully present and engaged during these activities, giving children undivided attention.

For example, a father might use the time driving their child to school as an opportunity to talk about the child's day, discuss their interests, or share stories. These moments of focused interaction can significantly enhance the father-child relationship.

Planning Special Activities:

Planning special activities tailored to the child's interests can create memorable bonding experiences. Fathers can organize weekend outings and family trips or participate in hobbies their child enjoys. Whether it's a trip to the park, a movie night, or a work project at home, these activities provide a break from the routine and offer a chance for fathers and children to create shared memories.

It's important for fathers to involve their children in planning these activities, giving them a sense of ownership and excitement. This collaborative approach not only makes the activities more enjoyable but also fosters a sense of partnership and mutual respect.

Embracing Spontaneity:

While planning is important, it is also important for fathers to embrace spontaneity and seize unexpected opportunities for quality time. Sometimes, the best moments are those that are unplanned, like a sudden rain shower that turns into a fun indoor game, a spontaneous dance party in the living room, or an impromptu baking session. Being open to these spontaneous moments and participating enthusiastically can create joyful and memorable experiences.

Making the Most of Limited Time:

For fathers with demanding work schedules, finding extensive periods for quality time can be challenging. However, even brief interactions can be meaningful if approached with intention and presence.

Focused Attention:

When time is limited, the quality of interaction matters more than the duration. Fathers need to strive to be fully present during the time they spend with their children, minimizing distractions like phone calls or work-related thoughts. This focused attention shows children they are a priority and that their father values their time together.

Active Engagement:

Active engagement involves participating wholeheartedly in activities and conversations. Whether it's helping with homework, playing a game, or simply talking about the day, fathers must focus on engaging with curiosity and enthusiasm. Asking questions, showing interest, and providing feedback make the interaction more enriching and meaningful.

Consistency:

Consistency is key to building trust and connection. Regular, even if brief, quality interactions create a sense of reliability and stability for children. As parents, fathers must aim to establish regular routines or rituals that involve quality time.

Active involvement in parenting is an expansive chapter in the subject of fatherhood that requires balancing work and personal life, overcoming challenges in bonding, and finding quality time for meaningful connections. Each of these components is integral to building a strong, supportive, and nurturing father-child relationship. Fathers must recognize the importance of their role in their children's lives and make conscious efforts to allocate time for family activities. Effective time management, setting boundaries, and prioritizing self-care are essential strategies for achieving this balance, serving as the fertile soil that allows it to thrive.

Finding quality time for meaningful connections goes beyond mere presence; it involves engaging in activities that curate deeper connections and shared experiences. Creating opportunities for quality time through daily routines, special activities, or spontaneous moments is crucial for nurturing a strong emotional bond. Even brief interactions can be impactful if approached with intention, focused attention, and active engagement.

Active involvement in parenting is about being present, engaged, and committed to building a loving and supportive relationship with children. By embracing these elements into their role, fathers can make a lasting positive impact on their children's lives, fostering their development, well-being, and happiness.

Chapter 9: Positive Guidance and Discipline

Over the ages, the importance of discipline has always been a key aspect of raising children, but its definition has changed with societal reformations. Now, a strategic approach is required to guide children since the role of fatherhood and childhood has altered. The aspect of effective discipline is the soul of parenting, aimed at guiding children toward acceptable behavior and instilling a sense of responsibility and self-control.

Many fathers struggle with finding the right balance between being too lenient and overly strict. In fact, ineffective discipline strategies can lead to a host of problems for both the child and the broader society.

Impact of Inconsistent and Harsh Discipline:

Inconsistency in enforcing rules and consequences can lead to confusion and insecurity in children. When children do not know what to expect from their parents, they may test boundaries more frequently, leading to behavioral issues. Studies show that inconsistent discipline is associated with higher levels of child anxiety and behavioral problems (Hentges et al., 2018).

On the other hand, harsh discipline practices, such as yelling, severe punishments, or physical discipline, can have detrimental effects on children's development. Harsh discipline is linked to increased aggression, antisocial behavior, and mental health issues such as depression and anxiety (Gershoff, 2013). Children subjected to harsh discipline may also develop poor relationships with their parents, leading to long-term relational and emotional issues.

Failing to acknowledge and reward positive behavior can also be problematic. Without positive reinforcement, children may not understand which behaviors are desirable and may feel unappreciated, leading to a lack of motivation to adhere to rules or meet expectations (Zolotor et al., 2008).

Fathers often bring a different perspective and set of approaches compared to mothers, contributing to a well-rounded parenting strategy. However, societal expectations and personal upbringing can influence how fathers discipline their children. Traditional notions of masculinity may pressure fathers to adopt a more authoritarian style, which can be counterproductive.

On the other hand, single fathers face additional challenges in disciplining their children. Without a partner to share the responsibilities and provide support, single fathers might struggle with maintaining consistency and managing stress. This can lead to either overly lenient or overly harsh discipline practices, both of which are detrimental to the child's well-being (Breivik & Olweus, 2006).

Effective Discipline Strategies for Fathers:

Given these challenges, it is essential for fathers to adopt effective and positive discipline strategies that promote healthy development and strong parent-child relationships. Here are some strategies to consider:

Setting Clear Expectations and Boundaries:

It is important for fathers to strive to be consistent in enforcing rules and consequences. This means applying the same rules and consequences every time a specific behavior occurs. Consistency helps children understand what is expected of them and builds a sense of security and trust.

It is important to communicate rules and expectations clearly. For fathers, it is essential to use simple, age-appropriate language to explain what behaviors are acceptable and why certain rules are in place. This helps children understand the rationale behind the rules and promotes compliance.

Rules should be tailored to the child's age and developmental stage. Younger children need simpler, more concrete rules, while older children can handle more complex expectations. Adjusting rules as children grow helps them learn and adapt appropriately.

Positive Reinforcement and Constructive Feedback:

Positive reinforcement involves acknowledging and rewarding good behavior. Fathers are encouraged to offer specific praise for positive actions, such as completing chores, showing kindness, or performing well in school. Tangible rewards, like treats or extra playtime, can also be effective motivators.

When addressing negative behavior, it is crucial to provide constructive feedback rather than harsh criticism. In their parenting journey, fathers must consider explaining why a behavior is unacceptable and offer guidance on how to improve.

This approach helps children learn from their mistakes without feeling discouraged or unloved.

Recognizing and praising the effort children put into tasks, rather than just the outcome, encourages a growth mindset. This teaches children that persistence and hard work are valuable, regardless of the immediate result.

Modeling Desired Behaviors:

Children learn a great deal by observing their parents. It is essential for fathers to model the behaviors and values they wish to instill in their children. Demonstrating respect, kindness, honesty, and integrity in everyday interactions sets a positive example for children to follow.

Fathers must ensure that their actions align with their words. Inconsistencies between what is said and what is done can confuse children and undermine the father's credibility.

Developing Emotional Intelligence:

Fathers need to strive to understand their children's emotions and perspectives. Showing empathy helps children feel heard and valued, reducing behavioral issues and strengthening the parent-child bond.

Teaching children how to manage their emotions is an important part of discipline. Fathers can help by modeling healthy emotional regulation and providing strategies for children to cope with strong emotions, such as deep breathing or taking a break to calm down.

Involving Children in the Process:

Involving children in the process of setting rules and consequences can increase their buy-in and compliance. Fathers can hold family meetings to discuss and agree on household rules, making children feel that their opinions are valued.

When issues arise, it is important for fathers to engage their children in problem-solving discussions. This approach teaches children to think critically and develop their own solutions, fostering independence and responsibility. Parenting requires a thoughtful balance of consistency, positive reinforcement, and empathy. Fathers are bestowed with a crucial role in this process, and adopting positive discipline strategies can lead to healthier, more respectful, and well-adjusted children.

Teaching Fundamental Values and Morals:

Teaching fundamental values and morals to children is one of the most important and challenging aspects of parenting. In today's fast-paced and ever-changing world, children are exposed to a wide range of influences, from peers and teachers to social media and pop culture.

These influences can sometimes contradict the values parents wish to instill, making the task even more daunting. For fathers, especially those who are single parents, the challenge of imparting strong moral foundations is intensified by the demands of balancing work, household responsibilities, and the need for quality time with their children.

Importance of Fundamental Values and Morals:

Values and morals serve as the guiding principles that shape a child's behavior, decision-making, and overall character. They curate the fundamentals of a person's identity and influence their interactions with others and their approach to life's challenges. Teaching children values such as honesty, respect, kindness, and responsibility helps them grow into conscientious adults and also contributes to the well-being of society as a whole.

Building a Strong Foundation:

Early Introduction: It is essential for fathers to start teaching values and morals at an early age. Even young children can grasp basic ideas of right and wrong, fairness, and empathy. Introducing these concepts early on helps ingrain them deeply into their consciousness, increasing the likelihood that they will follow them as they grow older.

Consistency: Consistency is key when teaching values. Children learn most effectively when they observe their parents consistently applying the same principles across different situations. For instance, regularly stressing the importance of honesty, even in minor matters, reinforces the value's significance.

Strategies for Teaching Values and Morals:

Fathers are powerful role models for their children, as discussed in previous chapters. Demonstrating the values and morals they wish to teach through their own actions is one of the most effective ways to impart these lessons. When children see their fathers acting with integrity, showing kindness, and taking responsibility, they are more likely to emulate these behaviors.

Whether it be in the form of stories or personal experiences, books, or cultural traditions, these mediums are excellent tools for teaching values. Fathers can use stories to illustrate the importance of various morals and the consequences of actions. These narratives can make abstract concepts more relatable and memorable for children.

Also, engaging children in open discussions about values and morals encourages them to think critically and form their own understanding. Fathers can use everyday situations as teachable moments, asking questions like, "What do you think is the right thing to do?" or "How would you feel if someone treated you that way?" These conversations help children internalize values and develop a moral compass.

Acknowledging and praising children when they exhibit positive values reinforces these behaviors. Fathers could provide specific praise, such as, "I'm proud of you for telling the truth," or "You showed great kindness by helping your friend." This recognition encourages children to continue acting in line with these values.

Fathers, as role models, must clearly communicate their expectations regarding behavior and the values they deem important. Establishing family rules based on these values provides a framework for children to follow. For instance, a rule about treating everyone with respect helps children understand and practice this value in their daily interactions.

Addressing Moral Dilemmas:

Children will inevitably face moral dilemmas as they grow. Fathers must be prepared to guide them through these challenges, helping them weigh the pros and cons of their choices and consider the ethical implications. Providing a safe space for children to discuss their dilemmas without fear of judgment encourages them to seek guidance and develop sound moral reasoning.

Teaching children to consider others' feelings and perspectives is a key component of moral development. Fathers can foster empathy by encouraging children to think about how their actions affect others and to practice kindness and compassion. Activities like volunteering or helping neighbors can provide practical opportunities for children to develop empathy.

Challenges for Single Fathers:

Balancing Roles: Fathers often juggle multiple roles, making it challenging to consistently teach and reinforce values. However, by prioritizing quality time and making the most of everyday interactions, fathers can effectively impart moral lessons. Finding support from extended family, friends, or community programs can also alleviate some of the burden and provide additional role models for children.

Managing Stress: The stress of single parenthood can sometimes lead to inconsistent discipline and moral teaching. This unmanaged stress can sometimes lead to addictions such as alcoholism and other harmful behaviors. One of my associates, Brian – a recovering alcoholic, described his situation to me, which in itself is a gutting story. He unraveled about how he has supervised visitation rights with his daughter.

He expressed to me the profound remorse he feels for missing out on so much of his daughter's formative years due to his addiction. Brian acknowledges his direct responsibility for his daughter's reluctance to see him and recognizes the disappointment he has caused both her and her mother. Filled with regret, he understands that he can never reclaim the lost years of his addiction. "Now that I am sober and can see clearly," he shared, "there's not a day that goes by that I don't hate myself for who I once was." He expressed his gratitude that his daughter's mother does not discourage their daughter from seeing him and allows her to decide on her own whether she wants to spend time with him.

Fathers need to find healthy ways to manage stress, such as exercise, hobbies, or seeking support from peers. A calm and focused approach to parenting helps create a stable environment conducive to moral development.

Creating a Support Network:

Fathers can benefit from creating a network of support that includes other parents, mentors, and community resources. This network can provide guidance, share experiences, and offer practical help, making it easier for fathers to consistently teach and reinforce values.

Teaching fundamental values and morals is a vital aspect of fatherhood that shapes a child's character and future. By employing strategies such as role modeling, storytelling, open discussions, positive reinforcement, and addressing moral dilemmas, fathers can effectively impart these crucial lessons.

Fathers can find it challenging to balance multiple roles and manage stress. However, with a strong support network and a focus on consistency, they can successfully instill strong moral foundations in their children.

Ultimately, the effort invested in teaching values and morals benefits individual children and contributes to creating a more ethical and compassionate society.

Role of Fathers in Shaping Behavior and Character:

Understanding the Issues:

The role of fathers in shaping their children's behavior and character is profound and complex. Fathers influence their children in various ways, from their daily interactions to the broader values and principles they instill. In today's society, children face numerous challenges and pressures that can impact their behavior and character development. Issues such as peer pressure, exposure to inappropriate content through media, and the stress of academic and extracurricular demands can all shape a child's behavior and character in ways that may not align with the values a father wishes to impart.

Facing Certain Challenges:

Peer Pressure: Children and adolescents often face significant peer pressure, which can lead them to engage in behaviors that are contrary to their family's values. Peer influence is particularly strong during the teenage years, and children may struggle to resist the pressure to conform to group norms, even when those norms conflict with their own moral compass.

Media Influence: The pervasive presence of media and technology in children's lives exposes them to a wide range of influences, some of which may potentially develop into a level of toxicity to which the child becomes exposed. From social media to television and video games, the content children consume can shape their attitudes and behaviors, often in subtle but significant ways.

Stress and Mental Health: The pressures of academic performance, extracurricular activities, and social dynamics can create stress and anxiety for children. These stressors can affect their behavior and character, leading to issues such as irritability, withdrawal, or risk-taking behaviors as they struggle to cope with their emotions.

Absence of Role Models: For single fathers, the absence of another parental figure can mean fewer role models for children to learn from. This can place additional pressure on the father to fulfill multiple roles and provide comprehensive guidance and support.

Strategies for Shaping Behavior and Character:

Despite these challenges, fathers have numerous strategies at their disposal to positively shape their children's behavior and character. Fathers can guide their children toward becoming responsible, ethical, and resilient individuals by providing a strong, consistent presence and employing thoughtful parenting techniques.

Leading by Example:

Modeling Desired Behaviors: Children learn a great deal from observing their parents. Fathers who consistently demonstrate honesty, integrity, compassion, and responsibility provide a powerful example for their children to follow. This modeling can be more impactful than verbal instructions, as children are more likely to imitate behaviors they see regularly.

Quality Time: Spending quality time with children is crucial for shaping their behavior and character. Engaging in activities together, whether it's playing sports, doing homework, or simply talking, helps fathers build strong bonds with their children. This connection makes children more receptive to their father's guidance and influence.

Listening and Understanding: Active listening is a critical component of effective parenting. It is important for fathers to make an effort to understand their children's thoughts, feelings, and perspectives. This not only fosters a supportive relationship but also helps fathers address any issues or concerns that may be influencing their children's behavior.

Setting Clear Expectations: When it comes to parenting, fathers should establish clear and reasonable expectations for their children's behavior. Fathers help children understand the importance of certain behaviors and the values they reflect by communicating these expectations and the reasons behind them. Clear expectations provide a framework for children to follow, which can guide their actions and decisions.

Encouraging Resilience: Teaching children how to handle setbacks and challenges is essential for their development.

Fathers can help their children develop resilience by encouraging them to view obstacles as opportunities for growth and learning. This perspective helps children build the emotional strength needed to navigate life's difficulties.

Problem-Solving Skills: Fathers can foster their children's problem-solving abilities by involving them in decision-making processes and guiding them through problem-solving steps. Teaching children to analyze situations, consider different solutions, and make thoughtful decisions equips them with skills that are valuable throughout life.

Understanding Underlying Causes: When children misbehave, it is important for fathers to understand the underlying causes of the behavior. Misbehavior can often be a sign of unmet needs, stress, or emotional struggles. By addressing the root causes, fathers can help their children find healthier ways to cope and behave.

Constructive Discipline: Instead of relying on punitive measures, fathers could use constructive discipline techniques that teach children the consequences of their actions and encourage better choices. Time-outs, loss of privileges, and firm and direct communications can be effective, provided they are used consistently and fairly.

Special Considerations for Single Fathers:

Balancing Multiple Roles: Single fathers must often balance multiple roles, from provider to caregiver and disciplinarian. Finding time for each role can be challenging, but prioritizing time with children and seeking support from extended family or community resources can help.

Nurturing Independence: Encouraging children to take on responsibilities and make decisions fosters independence and self-confidence. Fathers can support their children's development by providing opportunities for them to practice these skills in a safe and supportive environment.

The role of fathers in shaping their children's behavior and character is vital and complicated. By leading by example, spending quality time, encouraging positive behaviors, teaching resilience and problem-solving skills, and addressing misbehavior constructively, fathers can guide their children toward becoming responsible, ethical, and resilient individuals.

In conclusion, the role of fathers in shaping their children's behavior and character development is an irreplaceable factor. By leading through example, maintaining consistent involvement, and encouraging positive behaviors, fathers can help their children navigate life's challenges with confidence and integrity. Teaching values and morals require patience and dedication, but the rewards are significant, shaping children into responsible, ethical adults. Single fathers face unique challenges but can successfully impart these lessons by building support networks and finding a balance between their various roles.

Through active engagement, clear communication, and constructive discipline, fathers can foster resilience, empathy, and strong moral foundations in their children, ultimately contributing to the betterment of their families and communities.

Chapter 10: Fatherhood and Divorce/Separation/Death

Divorce is one of the most heart-wrenching experiences a family can endure. For certain fathers, the conclusion of a marriage can often be likened to losing a crucial piece of who they are. The separation brings with it a whirlwind of emotions—guilt, sorrow, confusion, and a profound sense of failure. Fathers might question their parenting role and effectiveness, wondering if they could have done more to keep the family together.

From the child's point of view, their familiar world is completely overturned. Young children may struggle to fully understand the consequences of divorce, which can cause them to feel fearful and confused. They might believe they are to blame, internalizing the conflict between their parents. Older children and teenagers, on the other hand, may feel anger and betrayal. They might withdraw or act out, struggling to process their emotions and the new reality they face.

These challenges are compounded equally for single fathers and mothers, who might not have a partner to share the emotional and logistical burdens of parenting. They often feel isolated and overburdened, juggling work, household responsibilities, and the needs of their children on their own. The absence of a partner means they have fewer opportunities to share the emotional labor, making it even more critical for them to find effective ways to cope and provide stability for their children.

Emotional Awareness and Self-Care: Fathers need to acknowledge their own feelings of grief, guilt, and loss. Seeking support from friends, family, or a therapist can provide a safe space to process these emotions.

Creating Stability and Routine: Children find comfort in routine and predictability. Establishing consistent visitation schedules and creating new family traditions can provide a sense of normalcy and security.

Open Communication: The aspect of open communication, as seen in previous chapters, has been vital in parenting. Encourage children to express their feelings and listen to them without judgment. Validating their emotions helps them process their experiences and reinforces their sense of being heard and understood.

Seeking Professional Help: Therapy can be beneficial for both fathers and children. A professional can offer strategies to cope with the emotional fallout of divorce and help rebuild the father-child relationship.

Building a Support Network: Fathers especially need a strong support network. Connecting with friends, family, or support groups can offer both practical assistance and emotional support.

By addressing these challenges head-on and implementing effective strategies, fathers can navigate the difficult terrain of divorce, providing their children with the stability, love, and support they need to heal and thrive. Despite the upheaval, these efforts help to foster resilience and maintain a strong, loving bond between father and child.

Maintaining Active Involvement Post-Divorce

Navigating the complexities of maintaining an active fatherly presence post-divorce requires dedication, empathy, and strategic planning. For fathers, the separation often means adjusting to new living arrangements and legal agreements while striving to sustain meaningful connections with their children. This phase demands emotional resilience and a proactive approach to mitigate the disruptive effects of divorce on family dynamics.

Let us take the example of Jason – a divorced man. Following his divorce, Jason faced the daunting challenge of preserving his role as a father to his two daughters, Nicole and Yvette. The court-mandated visitation schedule initially felt restrictive, with limited time slots that strained his efforts to maintain a consistent presence in their lives. Despite the logistical hurdles, Jason remained steadfast in prioritizing quality time with his daughters. He ensured that their visits were not merely passive moments but opportunities for genuine engagement and bonding.

Strategies for Maintaining Active Involvement:

Quality Over Quantity: Recognizing that the quantity of time spent together may be limited, focus on making every moment count. Engage in activities that foster shared interests and create lasting memories. For Jason, this meant organizing weekend outings to parks, museums, and local events where he could nurture their interests and strengthen their connection.

Consistency and Reliability: Establish a predictable routine that children can rely on. Consistency provides stability amidst the disturbance of divorce, reassuring children that despite the changes, their father remains a dependable presence in their lives. Jason made it a point to show up on time for visits, respecting their scheduled time together and demonstrating his commitment to being there for Nicole and Yvette.

Co-Parenting Cooperation: Collaborate with your ex-partner to prioritize the well-being of your children. Maintain respectful communication and work together to uphold consistent rules and routines across households. Jason and his ex-wife established a cooperative co-parenting relationship, exchanging important information about the girl's school activities, health needs, and emotional well-being.

Flexibility and Adaptability: Remain flexible in accommodating changes in schedules or unexpected events. Adaptability demonstrates your willingness to prioritize your children's needs above personal inconveniences. Jason adjusted his plans when necessary, rescheduling visits to accommodate Nicole and Yvette's school events or extracurricular activities, ensuring they felt supported and valued.

Maintaining active involvement post-divorce is a continuous journey of adjustment and growth for both father and child. By prioritizing quality time, consistency, open communication, cooperative co-parenting, and flexibility, fathers can mitigate the challenges of divorce and foster a resilient father-child relationship built on trust, love, and unwavering support. These efforts not only help children navigate the emotional complexities of divorce but also empower fathers to play an integral role in their children's lives, promoting their well-being and overall development despite the family's altered circumstances.

Impact of Divorce, Separation, or Death on Both Parent and Child

Impact on Fathers:

Emotional Turmoil: Fathers may experience a range of intense emotions, including sadness, anger, guilt, and loneliness. The loss of a partner disrupts their sense of stability and security, forcing them to confront the reality of single parenthood and its accompanying challenges.

Identity Crisis: The shift from being part of a couple to that of a single parent can trigger an identity crisis for both the father and mother. They may question their ability to fulfill both parental roles effectively, navigating feelings of self-doubt and uncertainty about their parenting capabilities.

Practical Challenges: Managing household responsibilities, financial obligations, and emotional support for children becomes daunting for single parents. Balancing work commitments with caregiving responsibilities requires strategic planning and resilience in the face of adversity.

Impact on Children:

Emotional Distress: Children often struggle to process the emotional upheaval caused by divorce, separation, or the death of a parent. They may exhibit signs of grief, anxiety, or depression, grappling with feelings of abandonment and insecurity.

Behavioral Changes: The loss of a parent or the disruption of family dynamics can manifest in behavioral changes among children. They may act out, withdraw socially, or exhibit academic difficulties as they try to cope with their emotions.

Loss of Stability: Divorce, separation, or death disrupts the familiar routines and sense of security that children rely on. They may feel unsettled and uncertain about the future, requiring reassurance and consistency from their parent to navigate the changes.

Strategies for Supporting Fathers and Children:

Encourage Expression: Foster open communication channels where fathers and children can discuss their feelings openly. Validate their emotions and reassure them that it's okay to grieve and seek support from each other. Make sure they understand that you're available for whatever they may need. Be the listening ear they can turn to when they're feeling sad, lonely, or confused.

Seek Support Networks: Connect with community resources, support groups, or counseling services to access guidance and emotional support. Sharing experiences with other fathers facing similar challenges can provide valuable insights and encouragement.

Promote Resilience: Encourage resilience-building activities, such as hobbies, sports, or creative outlets, to help children process their emotions and develop coping strategies. Celebrate their strengths and achievements to foster a positive outlook on their abilities.

Nurturing Father-Child Relationships in New Contexts:

The aftermath of divorce, separation, or the death of a partner often necessitates redefining father-child relationships within new familial contexts. For fathers, adjusting to co-parenting arrangements or single parenthood requires navigating uncharted waters while preserving the bonds that anchor their children's sense of security and belonging. This period demands flexibility, empathy, and a steadfast commitment to fostering meaningful connections despite the changed circumstances.

Consider the story of Adam, who faced the challenges of nurturing his relationship with his son, Tony, after divorcing Ethan's mother, April. The transition to shared custody meant that Adam's time with Tony was now structured and limited. Initially, Adam grappled with feelings of inadequacy and uncertainty about his role in Tony's life. Now, he worried that the physical distance and altered routines would strain their bond, impacting Tony's emotional well-being.

Challenges Faced by Fathers:

Navigating Co-Parenting Dynamics: Collaborating with an ex-partner to co-parent effectively requires navigating potential conflicts and maintaining open lines of communication. Differences in parenting styles or unresolved emotions from the divorce can complicate efforts to create a cohesive parenting approach that prioritizes the child's best interests.

Establishing New Routines: Adjusting to new visitation schedules or living arrangements requires fathers to establish predictable routines that provide stability and consistency for their children. This process involves negotiating logistical challenges while ensuring that quality time is prioritized for bonding and emotional support.

Emotional Resilience: Fathers may experience emotional challenges, such as grief over the loss of the family unit or feelings of guilt about the impact on their children. Processing these emotions and maintaining a positive outlook will be essential in developing a level of resiliency and adapting to the new familial dynamics.

Strategies for Nurturing Father-Child Relationships:

Prioritize Quality Time: Make the most of the time spent together by engaging in activities that foster connection and create shared experiences.

Listen Actively: Practice active listening to understand your child's thoughts, feelings, and concerns. Create a safe space for open communication where your child feels heard and validated. By demonstrating empathy and attentiveness, fathers can build trust and reinforce their supportive role in their child's life.

Celebrate Milestones: Acknowledge and celebrate important milestones, achievements, and special occasions in your child's life. Whether it's a birthday, academic success, or personal growth, recognize their accomplishments to instill a sense of pride and encouragement.

Flexibility and Adaptability: Remain flexible in responding to your child's evolving needs and preferences. Adapt to changes in routines or circumstances with patience and understanding, demonstrating your commitment to supporting their emotional well-being.

For Adam, fostering a nurturing relationship with Tony meant embracing the challenges of co-parenting with April while prioritizing Tony's emotional needs. He established a routine that balanced structured time with spontaneous moments of bonding, ensuring that their relationship flourished despite the separation. By maintaining open communication and demonstrating unwavering support, Adam reassured Tony of his steadfast presence in his life, approaching post-divorce dynamics with determination and compassion.

Navigating the complexities of nurturing father-child relationships in new contexts requires fathers to approach challenges with empathy, adaptability, and a proactive commitment to fostering meaningful connections. Despite the changes brought about by divorce, separation, or loss, fathers can play a vital role in supporting their children's emotional well-being and maintaining strong and robust family bonds.

The journey of navigating father-child relationships through the trials of divorce, separation, or loss is a testament to the commitment and compassion of fathers. It's a path marked by emotional complexity and practical challenges, where fathers must navigate new roles and dynamics with sensitivity and empathy.

Throughout this exploration, we've witnessed how fathers strive to maintain stability and emotional support for their children amidst significant life changes. The strategies discussed in this chapter underscore the importance of empathy and dedication in shaping family dynamics. Fathers who approach their roles with compassion create safe spaces for their children to express themselves, seek guidance, and find solace during times of uncertainty.

As fathers navigate the challenges of relationships after divorce or separation, they should find strength in their ability to provide unwavering love and support. Every interaction, no matter how small, adds to the ongoing story of fatherhood—a story that shapes their children's emotional world and leaves a lasting impact.

In embracing the challenges and joys of fatherhood in its true sense, fathers pave the way for deeper connections and meaningful relationships that endure beyond life's challenges. Let's acknowledge and honor the significant impact fathers have in nurturing resilient, compassionate individuals, shaping a legacy of love and empathy that surpasses challenges and ignites hope for future generations.

Chapter 11: Fatherhood and Incarceration

For a father on the journey of true fatherhood, incarceration means losing the opportunity to be a pillar of support in their children's lives. It denies him the chance to teach and guide by example, serving as a role model. In this painful absence, children may sometimes develop feelings of resentment toward their father.

Incarcerated fathers and mothers face numerous challenges in embracing the true role of parenthood. This chapter serves as a guide to help incarcerated fathers navigate these challenges and fulfill their roles more effectively.

Challenges of Being an Incarcerated Father:

Incarceration imposes a heavy burden not only on those serving time but also on their families, particularly their children. For fathers behind bars, the experience is laden with a unique set of challenges that significantly affect their ability to fulfill their paternal role. These challenges stem from physical separation, emotional strain, and the stigma associated with imprisonment.

Physical Separation:

The most immediate and tangible challenge is the physical separation between incarcerated fathers and their children. This distance disrupts the daily routines and interactions that form the backbone of parental relationships. Fathers miss out on significant milestones such as birthdays, school achievements, and everyday moments that nurture bonding.

This issue is not exclusive to incarcerated parents; it also affects those in the military who are deployed for extended periods. The prolonged absence can cause children to feel abandoned, leading to feelings of resentment toward the absent parent. While this situation is challenging for the children, the parents endure even greater pressure, carrying a burden they have no choice but to bear.

There's the case of Janet, one of my associates, who's an active-duty sailor and has been on multiple deployments, each lasting over the span of seven months. She described the heart-wrenching experience of seeing her two children crying on the pier as her ship departed. "It felt like my heart was being ripped out of my body," she said, vocalizing the emotions she felt at that moment. "Leaving my children behind is the hardest thing I've ever done in my life," she continued.

Even with a husband at home caring for her children, she couldn't escape the feeling of abandonment that gripped her heart. The choice was difficult as she described how she hated choosing between defending her country and leaving her children behind.

In other cases where single parents are presented with such choices, they find themselves at a junction where both choices are the ones no one would normally prefer. The lack of physical presence makes it difficult for fathers or mothers to provide the hands-on care and support that children need, leading to feelings of disconnection and abandonment that abolish the concept of fatherhood/parenthood from the children's lives.

Emotional Strain:

The emotional toll on incarcerated fathers is immense. They often experience feelings of guilt, shame, and helplessness, knowing that their actions could have contributed to their separation from their children. This emotional burden is compounded by the limited opportunities for meaningful interaction. The prison environment, characterized by strict routines and limited personal freedom, exacerbates feelings of isolation and depression. For many fathers, the inability to fulfill their paternal responsibilities weighs heavily on their mental health, affecting their overall well-being.

Communication Troubles:

Effective communication is another major hurdle for incarcerated fathers. The prison system imposes significant restrictions on communication, limiting phone calls, letters, and visitation rights. These barriers make it challenging to maintain consistent and meaningful contact with children. Monitored and brief phone calls or short visits in sterile, non-child-friendly environments can feel inadequate and intimidating. The lack of privacy and the controlled nature of communication can stifle genuine emotional exchanges, further straining the relationship.

Heavy Stigma:

Incarceration carries a heavy stigma that affects both the father and his family. Children of incarcerated parents often face bullying, social exclusion, and judgment from their peers and community. This stigma can lead to feelings of shame and embarrassment, making it difficult for children to talk openly about their father's situation.

For the incarcerated father, the awareness of this stigma adds to their emotional burden, knowing that their children are also suffering. The societal judgment extends to post-incarceration life, complicating reintegration efforts and the reestablishment of a stable family environment.

Financial Hardships:

Incarceration can often result in significant financial strain for families. The loss of the father's income can lead to economic instability, making it difficult to meet basic needs and maintain a stable home environment. This financial pressure can exacerbate stress and anxiety for both the incarcerated father and the family left behind. The expenses of maintaining contact through phone calls, visits, and adding funds to an inmate's account can increase the financial strain, making it even more difficult to manage.

Impact on Child Development:

The absence of a father significantly affects a child's development. Children may experience emotional and behavioral problems, academic struggles, and difficulties in forming healthy relationships. The lack of a positive male role model can lead to issues with self-esteem and identity.

The trauma of separation, combined with the stigma of having an incarcerated parent, can create long-lasting psychological impacts, leading them on a path of depression and suppressed emotional confidence. These challenges underscore the importance of maintaining father-child connections, even in the face of incarceration.

Legal and Custodial Issues:

Legal and custodial issues further complicate the situation for incarcerated fathers. Navigating custody arrangements, visitation rights, and maintaining parental responsibilities from behind bars can be daunting. Legal battles and the involvement of child protective services may arise, adding to the emotional and financial strain on the family. Fathers might struggle to assert their parental rights and stay involved in their children's lives, leading to feelings of powerlessness and frustration.

Incarceration brings about a series of trials for a parent, whether they are a mother or a father, affecting the nurturing of their children. While these challenges persist, they create even greater stress and instability in the case of single parents. However, there are ways for parents, particularly fathers, to embrace their role and remain involved, even in such difficult circumstances.

Supporting Incarcerated Fathers

Addressing the needs of incarcerated fathers involves providing emotional support, practical assistance, and opportunities to remain involved in their children's lives. A multifaceted approach helps mitigate the negative impact of incarceration on family dynamics and facilitates the maintenance of meaningful connections.

Emotional Support:

Providing emotional support to incarcerated fathers is crucial in helping them navigate the psychological challenges of imprisonment. This support can come from mental health professionals, support groups, and family members who offer a listening ear and encouragement. Acknowledging and addressing their emotional struggles can help fathers remain resilient and maintain hope for the future.

Parenting Programs:

Many correctional facilities offer parenting programs that equip incarcerated fathers with skills and strategies to stay connected with their children. These programs often include parenting classes, communication workshops, and resources for maintaining emotional bonds despite physical separation. Participating in these programs enables fathers to learn to express love and support in ways that resonate with their children even if they aren't actively present in their lives.

Visitation and Communication:

Facilitating regular visitation and communication is essential in maintaining father-child relationships. Correctional facilities can play a significant role by providing child-friendly visitation environments and allowing for more frequent and meaningful interactions. While some facilities may have strict rules regarding this luxury, harnessing whatever time they offer to show their presence in their children's lives is essential for fathers. Also, encouraging letter writing and phone and video calls can help sustain emotional connections and keep fathers involved in their children's lives.

Building a Support Network:

Connecting incarcerated fathers with a support network can make a significant difference in their ability to maintain and strengthen family ties. Support networks might include fellow inmates who share similar experiences, family members who can provide emotional backing, and community organizations dedicated to supporting families affected by incarceration. These networks can offer practical advice, emotional encouragement, and a sense of solidarity that helps fathers feel less isolated.

Legal and Logistical Assistance:

Navigating the legal and logistical challenges of maintaining family connections from prison can be overwhelming. Providing incarcerated fathers with access to legal advice and assistance can help them understand their rights and options for maintaining contact with their children. Additionally, logistical support, such as help with arranging visits and coordinating communication, can alleviate some of the practical barriers to staying connected.

Educational and Vocational Training:

Investing in the education and vocational training of incarcerated fathers has the potential to have a ripple effect on their ability to provide for their families and serve as role models. Programs that offer GED preparation, college courses, or vocational skills training enhance the fathers' prospects upon release and also send a message to their children about the importance of education and self-improvement. While it serves a purpose for the fathers, it may also be perceived by children as a positive activity, leading to uplifting the father's image in their eyes and perception.

Therapeutic Interventions:

Therapeutic interventions, such as counseling and therapy sessions, can be vital in helping incarcerated fathers address underlying issues that may have contributed to their incarceration. These interventions provide a safe space to explore personal challenges, develop coping strategies, and prepare for a healthier reentry into family life. Therapy can also facilitate better communication skills, which are essential for maintaining and rebuilding relationships with children.

On the other hand, children with incarcerated parents should be encouraged to join a therapy session to navigate through the complexities of the array of emotions that they may be facing. In many cases, the co-partner could step up into this role and ensure that the child's welfare is a priority.

However, if, for some reason, the co-partner isn't available or in the case of a single parent who is incarcerated, therapy sessions are vital for the children, especially when they have to face societal and personal challenges.

Collaboration with Caregivers:

Cooperation and open communication with the caregivers of their children, whether they are the children's mother, grandparents, or other relatives, are crucial for incarcerated fathers. Establishing a collaborative relationship ensures that everyone involved is working toward the common goal of the child's well-being. Sharing information about the child's development, challenges, and achievements helps incarcerated fathers stay informed and feel more connected to their children's lives.

Programs Focused on Reentry:

Programs that prepare incarcerated fathers for reentry into society can include components specifically designed to address family reintegration. These programs might cover topics such as parenting after incarceration, managing family expectations, and dealing with the emotional complexities of returning home. By addressing these issues before release, fathers can approach reentry with a clearer understanding of the steps needed to rebuild their relationships with their children.

Supporting incarcerated fathers involves a comprehensive strategy that addresses emotional, educational, logistical, and therapeutic needs. Providing these resources and opportunities can help these fathers maintain meaningful connections with their children, laying the groundwork for stronger family bonds and better outcomes upon release. This will also require that the father ensure they are doing their part to ensure that they do not repeatedly find themselves back in the same situation.

Rebuilding Father-Child Bonds After Incarceration:

Rebuilding father-child bonds after incarceration is a critical process that requires time, effort, and empathy. The period of separation often leaves emotional scars on both the father and the children, making the journey toward reconnection a delicate and essential task. This process is not only about resuming physical presence but also about healing emotional wounds and re-establishing trust and mutual understanding.

Understanding the Emotional Impact:

Upon release, fathers must confront the emotional impact of their absence on their children. Children may harbor feelings of abandonment, resentment, or confusion. The sudden reappearance of a father can be jarring, especially if the children have adapted to life without him.

Acknowledging these emotions is the first step toward rebuilding bonds. Fathers need to understand that their children might have developed coping mechanisms or formed attachments to other caregivers during their absence. So, instead of using force and harsh love to get accepted by children, fathers should approach them with love and care. It's like renovating a worn-out house that requires patience and dedication to be restored to its original state.

Building Healthy Relationships:

Trust is the heart of any healthy relationship, and rebuilding it after incarceration requires patience and consistency. Children need to see that their fathers are reliable and committed to being a positive presence in their lives.

This trust is rebuilt through consistent actions, such as keeping promises, being present for important events, and actively listening to their children's concerns and feelings. It's essential for fathers to show that they are genuinely invested in their children's well-being and are committed to being there for them.

Re-establishing Communication:

This is the core element for rebuilding bonds. Fathers should approach conversations with openness, honesty, and a willingness to listen. It's important to create a safe space where children feel comfortable expressing their feelings without fear of judgment. They may have complaints or pent-up anger due to hearing countless taunts from their peers, which they need to let out. In the face of such situations, patience, active listening, and a calm expression of their point of view may be effective.

Fathers should share their experiences, apologize for their absence, and explain their efforts to improve. They should also allow themselves to be open enough to own up to the faults that they've made. Honest communication helps children understand their father's journey and fosters a deeper emotional connection.

Setting Realistic Expectations:

Rebuilding relationships takes time, and it's crucial to set realistic expectations. Fathers should understand that their children may not immediately welcome them back with open arms. There may be a period of adjustment, and setbacks are natural. Patience is key, as rushing the process can lead to further strain. Imagine the process of regrowing a garden that has wilted due to the gardener's absence.

Fathers should focus on gradual progress, celebrating small victories, and recognizing that building strong bonds is a long-term endeavor.

Creating Positive Experiences:

Shared experiences can significantly strengthen father-child bonds. Fathers should seek opportunities to engage in meaningful activities with their children, such as playing games, helping with homework, or participating in hobbies. These moments create positive memories and reinforce the emotional connection. Engaging in activities that the children enjoy shows that their interests and happiness are a priority.

Seeking Professional Support:

In some cases, professional support can facilitate the process of rebuilding bonds. Family counseling or therapy provides a structured environment for addressing underlying issues and improving communication. Therapists can help fathers and children navigate the complex emotions associated with incarceration and reintegration. Professional guidance ensures that both parties have the tools they need to heal and build a stronger relationship.

Addressing Behavioral Challenges:

Children may exhibit behavioral challenges as a result of the emotional turmoil caused by their father's absence. Fathers should approach these challenges with compassion and understanding. Rather than resorting to strict discipline, they should seek to understand the root causes of the behavior and work collaboratively to find solutions. Addressing behavioral issues with patience and compassion helps build trust and fosters a supportive environment.

Modeling Positive Behavior:

Children learn by observing their parents. Fathers should strive to model positive behavior, demonstrating qualities like responsibility, respect, and understanding. By setting a good example, fathers can positively influence their children's behavior and character and can rebuild their image in front of them. Showing a consistent effort to improve oneself and being a positive role model can inspire children and strengthen the father-child relationship. Rebuilding father-child bonds after incarceration is important and will require determination, patience, and trust. By approaching this process with compassion, endurance, and a commitment to positive change, fathers can heal emotional wounds, re-establish trust, and build strong, lasting relationships with their children.

One of the most important things an incarcerated father or mother can do is to own their mistakes. Show their remorse and acknowledge the faults that led them to where they are now. This honesty and truthfulness can sometimes mend relationships in ways that denying their actions and constantly portraying themselves as blameless cannot. Children often seek answers to the taunts and frustrations they face, and expressing remorse for the mistakes that led to a parent's incarceration can help heal some of these wounds. This acknowledgment can instill hope for a better future as they come to realize that things may change when their mother or father returns home.

"Do the best you can until you know better. Then, when you know better, do better."

~ Maya Angelou

Chapter 12: Fatherhood as a Single Parent

The journey of fatherhood, though filled with its own beauty, can sometimes be complex and challenging, but the path becomes even more demanding when a man finds himself navigating this role alone. Balancing the empathetic and nurturing aspects of motherhood with the duties of fatherhood can overwhelm a father's ability to live up to the ideal vision of fatherhood they initially envisioned.

Reasons Leading to Single Parenting:

The reasons why a father might end up as a single parent are varied and often deeply personal. Divorce, the death of a partner, unplanned pregnancies, or situations where the mother is unable or unwilling to take on the parenting role can all result in single fatherhood. Each scenario brings its own set of emotional and logistical challenges, compelling these fathers to adapt swiftly to their new responsibilities.

Divorce:

Divorce is a common reason why many fathers find themselves in the role of a single parent. The dissolution of a marriage can be a traumatic experience, not only for the couple but also for their children. Fathers who become single parents through divorce often face the challenge of maintaining a sense of normalcy and stability for their children amidst the disruption. They can find themselves consumed by juggling co-parenting arrangements, legal battles, and the emotional fallout of the separation. This can be a profoundly isolating experience, as the support system that once included a partner is no longer there, leaving the father to shoulder the emotional and practical responsibilities alone.

Partner's Death:

The death of a partner is another heartbreaking reason why a father might end up as a single parent. The sudden or anticipated loss of a spouse brings overwhelming grief and a sense of profound loss. In addition to coping with their own sorrow, fathers find themselves climbing through that narrow cliff of grief to avert their focus on supporting their children through the grieving process. They are tasked with being the emotional rock for their family while managing their own pain. The absence of the partner leaves a void that is felt deeply in the day-to-day life of the family, from the big moments to the small routines that once were shared. In this situation, single fathers often face the dual burden of mourning and the practicalities of managing a household alone.

There is the case of Robert, who's steering through the life of a single parent of two children – a nine-year-old daughter and a seven-year-old son. Two years ago, his world fell apart when he lost his partner in a tragic car accident. Suddenly, he was left to face the indescribable loss on his own.

Robert described the trauma of losing his wife and the immense impact it had on his and his children's lives. Overnight, his world had changed as he found himself being thrust into the challenging role of a single caregiver. Although he had been deeply involved in his children's lives, the responsibilities of being a single father had alternated the whole landscape of his vision as he found himself marching into uncharted territory.

Unplanned Pregnancy:

Unplanned pregnancies can also act as the catalyst to leading toward single fatherhood. In some cases, the mother may be unable or unwilling to take on the parenting role, leaving the father as the primary caregiver. This scenario can be especially challenging if the father is not initially prepared for the responsibilities of parenthood. These fathers may face societal judgment and a lack of support as they step into a role they may not have anticipated. The sudden shift in lifestyle and priorities can be daunting, requiring rapid adaptation and a steep learning curve. Despite these challenges, many single fathers rise to the occasion, demonstrating remarkable resilience and dedication.

Unreliable Partner:

In situations where the mother is unable to parent due to issues such as addiction, mental health problems, incarceration, or physical disabilities, fathers are left with no choice but to step in as the primary caregiver. These scenarios often come with their own set of complexities. Single fathers in this situation are faced with a rough hand dealt by fate as they must manage not only their own responsibilities but also the additional stress of dealing with the mother's circumstances. They might face financial strain, social stigma, and the emotional burden of explaining the situation to their children. Despite these challenges, many fathers in this position go to great lengths to provide a stable and loving environment for their children.

Personal Choice:

While there are reasons that lead a father or a parent to the stage of single parenting, this situation can also arise from conscious choice. Some men choose to become single fathers through adoption, surrogacy, or other means. Though determined to be a father at first, they often face a unique set of challenges as they navigate the legal and logistical hurdles of becoming a single parent. Encountering societal biases and a lack of understanding about their choice can bring ripples of second thoughts in their once resolute mindset.

Each of these scenarios brings its own set of challenges, but they also highlight the diverse pathways that can lead to single fatherhood. Regardless of the circumstances, single fathers share a common bond of resilience, adaptability, and dedication to their children. The journey of single fatherhood is fraught with difficulties, finding the balance of adopting the motherly traits in their fatherly nature, but it is also marked by moments of profound love, joy, and fulfillment.

Unique Challenges Faced by Single Fathers:

The intricacies of single fatherhood are intertwined with a host of unique challenges, many of which can feel overwhelming, casting a shadow of stress and anxiety in the father's mind.

Societal Perception:

One of the most pressing issues is the societal perception and stereotypes surrounding single fathers. In many cultures, the primary caregiving role has traditionally been associated with mothers, leading to the misconception that men are less capable of nurturing and raising children. This cultural bias can result in single fathers facing undue scrutiny and skepticism regarding their parenting abilities. They often have to work harder to prove themselves as competent caregivers to family, friends, and even institutions like schools and healthcare providers. This constant need to validate their role can be exhausting and demoralizing.

Finding the Balance between Work and Parenting:

Balancing work and parenting is another significant challenge for single fathers. The dual responsibility of being the primary provider and the main caregiver creates a tightrope that requires careful navigation. Many single fathers struggle to find adequate childcare that aligns with their work schedules, which can lead to difficult choices about employment and career progression. The lack of flexible work arrangements and parental leave options tailored to single fathers further exacerbates this issue. These fathers often find themselves in a cycle of perpetual fatigue, trying to meet the demands of their jobs while also being present and engaged in their children's lives.

Financial Burden:

Financial strain is a common concern for single fathers. Without the support of a partner, they bear the full weight of financial responsibilities, including housing, utilities, food, healthcare, and education. The pressure to provide a stable and secure environment for their children can be immense, especially if the father's income is limited. Single fathers may also face additional expenses related to childcare, legal fees from custody arrangements, and the cost of activities and necessities for their children. This financial burden can lead to anxiety and stress, making it difficult to focus on the emotional and developmental needs of their children.

Wavering Emotional Health:

The emotional toll of single fatherhood cannot be understated. The absence of a partner means that single fathers often lack a confidant with whom they can share the highs and lows of parenting. This isolation can lead to feelings of loneliness and depression as they navigate the challenges of raising children without the emotional support of a partner.

Sometimes, the absence of a father figure from the parent's own life leaves them with a void that they carry along with them for the rest of their lives. Like Sydney, a married father with a child opened up to me about his upbringing marked by hardship and trauma. Raised by a single parent with his father absent, Sydney shared how he felt the void of paternal presence throughout his childhood, often blaming himself for his father's absence and feeling unloved. I related to Sydney's experience, sharing that my own father was absent during my upbringing, leading me to similar feelings of abandonment and longing for paternal guidance. Although my mother did her best to nurture and support me, I deeply longed for a father figure to guide me through the challenges of growing into manhood, offering both a role model and a source of love and support.

This is why single fathers must navigate their own grief and loss, whether from the end of a relationship, the death of a partner, or other circumstances that led to single parenthood. Balancing their emotional well-being with their children's needs demands tremendous strength and resilience.

Sydney explained that growing up without a father made him realize the crucial importance of a father's role. Now that he is a father, he is committed to always being present in his child's life, even if he and his spouse should ever separate.

Fluctuations in Daily Life:

Parenting as a single father also involves managing the logistics of daily life. The responsibilities can feel endless, from coordinating school drop-offs and pickups to managing extracurricular activities, medical appointments, and household chores. The lack of a partner to share these tasks means that single fathers must become adept at multitasking and time management. They often have to prioritize and make sacrifices to ensure that their children's needs are met, which can leave little time for self-care and personal interests.

Despite these challenges, single fathers display remarkable resilience and determination. They adapt to their circumstances with creativity and resourcefulness, finding ways to overcome obstacles and provide a loving and stable environment for their children. The journey of single fatherhood is not without its difficulties but is filled with moments of profound connection, growth, and joy. Through their unwavering commitment and love, single fathers demonstrate that they are more than capable of raising happy, healthy, and well-adjusted children.

Nurturing Resilience and Adaptability in Fatherhood:

Single fatherhood requires a profound reservoir of resilience and adaptability as challenges attached to it are perilous to their mental and emotional health. Fathers who find themselves raising children alone must develop these traits not only to navigate the practicalities of everyday life but also to foster a nurturing environment that promotes their children's emotional and psychological well-being. The path of single fatherhood is marked by a continuous need to adapt, learn, and grow, often under challenging circumstances. Yet, it is within these very challenges that the seeds of resilience and adaptability are sown.

The Aspect of Resilience:

Resilience in single fathers is often forged through the daily trials and tribulations of solo parenting. Every day presents new hurdles, from managing household chores and financial responsibilities to providing emotional support and guidance. Single fathers must cultivate an inner strength that allows them to face these challenges head-on without the immediate support of a partner.

This resilience is not just about enduring hardships; it is about thriving despite them. It involves maintaining a positive outlook, finding creative solutions to problems, and refusing to be defeated by setbacks. By embodying resilience, single fathers become powerful role models for their children, demonstrating that adversity can be overcome with determination and perseverance.

Necessity of Adaptability:

Adaptability is equally crucial in the landscape of single fatherhood. The ability to pivot and adjust to changing circumstances is a skill that single fathers must master. Parenting, in any form, is unpredictable, and single fathers often find themselves having to quickly adapt to new routines, unexpected events, and evolving needs of their children. This might mean rearranging work schedules to attend school events, finding alternative childcare solutions on short notice, or learning new skills to support their children's development.

In the case of Robert, the sudden shouldering of responsibility for filling both parental roles made him adapt quickly to this new dynamic. This transformation underscored for him the critical importance of his position in his children's lives, not just as a father but as a guiding force in their development and growth. He experienced firsthand the rewards and challenges that came with his role, realizing the profound impact he had on his children's lives.

It doesn't mean you have to carry the burden alone and adapt to the tribulations that arise. Adaptability also means being open to seeking help and accepting support when needed, whether from family, friends, or community resources. It involves a willingness to learn and grow alongside their children, embracing new roles and responsibilities with a flexible outlook.

Factors Involved in Building Adaptability:

Emotional Resilience:

The emotional resilience of single fathers is another vital aspect of nurturing adaptability. Single fathers must navigate their own emotions while providing a stable and loving environment for their children. This often means processing feelings of grief, loss, or loneliness in healthy ways so that these emotions do not negatively impact their parenting. Fathers who openly express their emotions and seek support when needed are better able to model healthy emotional behaviors for their children. By showing their children that it is okay to feel and express a range of emotions, single fathers help foster an environment of emotional intelligence and security.

Curation of a Reliable Support Network:

Building resilience and adaptability also involves fostering a strong support network. Single fathers need a community of friends, family, and peers who can offer practical help, emotional support, and encouragement. This network can provide a safety net that helps fathers manage the demands of single parenthood. It can also offer valuable advice and shared experiences, helping single fathers feel less isolated in their journey. Engaging with other single parents, whether through local support groups or online communities, can provide a sense of camaraderie and shared understanding. Knowing that others have faced similar challenges and found ways to overcome them can be incredibly empowering and motivating.

Flourishing these traits in children is a critical aspect of single fatherhood. Under the influence of these qualities, children learn how to cope with change and uncertainty, equipping themselves with the skills to navigate life's ups and downs. This involves creating a stable and supportive home environment where children feel safe to express their feelings and explore their interests.

Fathers who adapt to the balance required on this new path can foster resilience by celebrating their children's achievements, no matter how small, and by providing comfort and guidance during challenging times, helping to fill the void left by their mother's absence. Striking the right balance between a father's discipline and a mother's love is crucial in nurturing their children. Teaching children problem-solving skills, fostering independence, and encouraging a growth mentality are all ways that single fathers can help their children develop resilience and adaptability.

At the heart of these qualities remain the unconditional love and commitment that single fathers bring to their role. Despite the challenges and sacrifices, single fathers should commit to demonstrating an unwavering dedication to their children's well-being. This love and commitment create a foundation of trust and security, enabling children to feel confident and supported as they navigate their own paths.

The bond between a single father and his children is strengthened through shared experiences, open communication, and mutual respect – the qualities essential in the journey of fatherhood, as discussed in the previous chapters. This bond not only helps children thrive but also strengthens the father's resilience and adaptability, creating a positive cycle of mutual support and strength.

Single fatherhood is a challenging path in the journey of parenting that requires a deep understanding of their role, a willingness to adjust, and the most important element of all – love, to guide them toward a better path. By cultivating qualities like determination and flexibility, single fathers develop the ability to create nurturing environments where their children can thrive. They lead by example, demonstrating that challenges can be faced with courage and creativity and that persistence and hope builds endurance.

To be a successful single father, it's essential to manage the weight of these demanding responsibilities by engaging in support groups, practicing patience in their emotional journey, and staying dedicated to their role. By embracing fatherhood with empathy, single fathers can overcome their own challenges and inspire their children to grow into confident, emotionally stable individuals ready to face the world with strength.

The journey may be filled with dark moments and challenges, but regardless of the circumstances, how they see themselves, or how society perceives them, fathers should remember that, in their children's eyes, they are still their dad. It may take time, but with a strong and determined heart, every obstacle can be faced and overcome.

"Being a single parent is twice the work, twice the stress, and twice the tears. But also, twice the hugs, twice the love, and twice the pride."

Chapter 13: Cultural and Global Perspectives on Fatherhood

Fatherhood, while a universal concept, manifests differently across various cultures, reflecting unique societal values, traditions, and expectations. These cultural variations influence how fathers engage with their children and families, shaping the roles they play and the methods they use to provide care and support. Understanding these diverse perspectives allows us to appreciate the richness of fatherhood and the ways in which cultural contexts shape paternal roles.

Fatherhood Across Different Cultures:

Western Cultures:

In Western cultures, particularly in North America and Europe, the role of the father has undergone significant transformation over the past few decades. Traditionally, Western fathers were primarily seen as breadwinners whose main responsibility was to provide financial support for the family (Seward et al., n.d.). Emotional caregiving and day-to-day child-rearing tasks were often relegated to mothers. However, contemporary Western society has seen a notable shift toward more involved and hands-on fatherhood.

Modern Western fathers are increasingly recognized for their role in nurturing and emotional support. They are actively involved in all aspects of child-rearing, from changing diapers and preparing meals to participating in school activities and fostering open communication. This shift reflects broader societal changes toward gender equality and the recognition that fathers play a crucial role in the emotional and psychological development of their children.

In many Western countries, policies and practices have evolved to support this shift. Paternity leave, flexible working hours, and shared parental leave are becoming more common, allowing fathers to spend more time with their newborns and share parenting responsibilities more equally with mothers. This has nurtured a more balanced approach to parenting, where both parents contribute to the upbringing and well-being of their children.

Asian Cultures:

In many Asian cultures, the role of the father is deeply rooted in tradition and social hierarchy. Fathers are often seen as the authoritative figures within the family, responsible for making important decisions and maintaining discipline. In countries like China, Japan, and India, the father's role traditionally involved ensuring the family's financial stability, instilling values, and guiding children toward academic and professional success. Their strictness in implementing these values in their children often resulted in the children being mentally strained or socially awkward – however, fathers had the final say in the household, and their decisions couldn't be challenged.

Despite these traditional views, there is a growing trend toward more involved and emotionally present fatherhood in Asia. Economic changes, globalization, and exposure to different cultural norms have influenced how fatherhood is perceived and practiced. For example, in Japan, the "ikumen" movement encourages men to take an active role in parenting, challenging the traditional notion of fathers as distant providers (Benedikt Brüning, 2020). This movement promotes the idea that fathers can and should be involved in caregiving, and it is supported by policies that offer paternity leave and encourage work-life balance.

In China, rapid economic development and urbanization have led to changes in family dynamics. Younger generations of fathers are more likely to engage in nurturing roles, influenced by both modern ideals and the practicalities of dual-income households. Similarly, in India, urban fathers are becoming more involved in day-to-day parenting tasks, moving away from the solely authoritative role traditionally assigned to them.

African Cultures:

African cultures present a rich compilation of fatherhood practices, often characterized by strong communal and extended family structures. In many African societies, the role of the father extends beyond the nuclear family, with fathers playing a crucial part in the upbringing of not just their biological children but also nieces, nephews, and other community children.

In countries like Nigeria, Kenya, and South Africa, fathers are seen as protectors, providers, and educators. They are responsible for imparting cultural values, traditions, and life skills to their children, ensuring the continuity of their heritage. This communal approach to fatherhood means that children benefit from the guidance and support of multiple father figures within the extended family and community. However, African fathers also face unique challenges, such as economic instability, political turmoil, and health crises, which can impact their ability to fulfill their roles.

Despite these challenges, many African fathers strive to maintain strong bonds with their children and provide for their families, often with the support of extended family networks.

Latin American Cultures:

In Latin American cultures, the concept of "machismo" has traditionally emphasized the father's role as a strong, authoritative figure. Fathers were expected to be the primary providers and protectors, often maintaining emotional distance to uphold their perceived strength and authority. However, there is a growing movement toward more nurturing and emotionally involved fatherhood in Latin America.

In countries like Brazil, Mexico, and Argentina, many fathers are challenging traditional stereotypes and embracing their role as caregivers and emotional supporters. This shift is reflected in increasing paternal involvement in daily caregiving tasks, such as feeding, bathing, and bedtime routines.

Latin American fathers are also becoming more vocal about their desire to be present and engaged in their children's lives. This change is driven by evolving societal norms, increased awareness of the importance of emotional bonds, and the influence of global movements toward gender equality. As a result, many Latin American families are experiencing a more balanced approach to parenting, where fathers play a central role in nurturing and supporting their children.

Indigenous Cultures:

Indigenous cultures worldwide offer unique perspectives on fatherhood, often emphasizing the spiritual and educational roles of fathers. In many indigenous communities, fathers are seen as vital teachers and role models, responsible for passing down cultural knowledge, traditions, and values to their children.

In Native American cultures, for example, fathers play a crucial role in teaching their children about their heritage, language, and traditional practices. They are involved in various ceremonies and rituals that reinforce cultural identity and community bonds. This deep connection to their cultural roots helps children develop a strong sense of identity and belonging.

Similarly, in Australian Aboriginal cultures, fathers are integral to the community's social and cultural fabric. They participate in storytelling, hunting, and other activities that transmit cultural knowledge and skills to their children. This involvement fosters a strong sense of community and continuity, ensuring that cultural traditions are preserved for future generations.

Evolved over the ages, fatherhood across different cultures highlights the diversity and complexity of paternal roles and responsibilities. While the specifics may vary, the core essence of fatherhood—providing love, support, guidance, and protection—remains universal. By appreciating and understanding these cultural differences, one can foster a more inclusive and supportive environment for fathers worldwide, recognizing their vital contributions to their families and communities.

Fathers' Role in Alternative Family Structures:

The concept of family is evolving, reflecting changes in societal norms, legal frameworks, and individual choices. Alternative family structures—such as single-parent families, blended families, LGBTQ+ families, and families formed through adoption or surrogacy—are becoming more common and accepted. Within these diverse configurations, the role of fathers continues to be vital, though it may manifest differently than in traditional nuclear families. Exploring these roles helps in understanding how fathers adapt and thrive in various family settings, providing stability, love, and support to their children.

Single-Parent Families:

In single-parent families, where fathers take on the primary caregiving role, they often face unique challenges and opportunities. Balancing work, household responsibilities, and parenting duties can be demanding, but single fathers also have the chance to form deep, one-on-one bonds with their children.

Single fathers may initially struggle with societal expectations that often view men as secondary caregivers. They are more vulnerable to encountering skepticism about their ability to manage household chores, provide emotional support, and maintain a nurturing environment. However, many single fathers rise to the occasion, demonstrating they can be just as capable and loving as any other parent.

Building a support network is crucial for single fathers. By actively seeking and accepting support, single fathers can create a stable and nurturing environment for their children.

Blended Families:

Blended families, formed when one or both partners bring children from previous relationships into a new union, present unique dynamics and challenges. Fathers in blended families must navigate the complexities of forming bonds with stepchildren while maintaining relationships with their biological children.

Establishing trust and respect is essential in blended families. Fathers can create positive relationships by being patient, understanding, and consistent. Open communication with both the partner and the children helps address concerns and set clear expectations. In these settings, fathers often play a crucial role in mediating conflicts and ensuring that all children feel valued and included.

Blended families benefit from creating new traditions and routines that include all family members. Fathers can lead by planning family activities that encourage bonding and cooperation. These efforts can help integrate the family and create a sense of unity despite the possible challenges.

LGBTQ+ Families:

In LGBTQ+ families, fathers may be part of same-sex couples or may identify as transgender. These families face unique societal pressures and legal challenges, but they also demonstrate resilience and strength in the face of adversity. Fathers in LGBTQ+ families play crucial roles in providing loving and supportive environments for their children.

Same-sex fathers often navigate legal and social systems that may not fully recognize their parental rights. Advocacy and legal action have led to greater recognition and protections for LGBTQ+ families, but challenges remain. Despite these challenges, many LGBTQ+ fathers develop deep, nurturing connections with their children, highlighting the universal nature of love and caregiving.

In transgender families, fathers may undergo gender transition while parenting. This journey can be complex, requiring open communication and sensitivity to the needs and emotions of the children. Fathers in these situations demonstrate courage and authenticity, teaching their children valuable lessons about identity, acceptance, and resilience.

Adoptive and Surrogate Families:

Adoptive and surrogate families highlight the diverse ways in which fathers can build and nurture families. These fathers often face unique challenges related to the adoption or surrogacy process, but their commitment to their children should remain unwavering.

Adoptive fathers may need to address issues of identity and belonging as their children navigate their backgrounds and histories. Open and honest communication about adoption, coupled with unconditional love and support, helps children understand their origins and feel secure in their family environment. Fathers in adoptive families play a critical role in fostering a sense of belonging and self-worth.

Surrogate fathers, particularly those in same-sex relationships or single-parent families, may face societal scrutiny or legal hurdles. However, the journey of surrogacy often strengthens their resolve and commitment to parenting. By embracing the process and openly discussing it with their children, surrogate fathers build strong foundations of trust and transparency.

In alternative family structures, fathers adapt to their unique circumstances, providing stability, love, and guidance to their children. Whether as single parents, part of blended families, members of LGBTQ+ communities, or in adoptive and surrogate families, fathers demonstrate resilience and commitment.

Their roles may vary, but the core essence of fatherhood—offering support, protection, and unconditional love—remains steadfast. By acknowledging and celebrating these diverse forms of fatherhood, we can foster a more inclusive understanding of family and recognize the vital contributions of fathers in all their forms.

Initiatives for Father-Inclusive Policies and Practices:

As society evolves, so does our understanding of the essential role fathers play in the development and well-being of their children. Historically, policies and practices often centered on mothers as primary caregivers, but there is a growing recognition of the importance of father involvement. This shift has led to the development of father-inclusive policies and practices designed to support and encourage active fatherhood. These initiatives aim to break down barriers, challenge stereotypes, and create an environment where fathers can thrive as equal partners in parenting.

Paternity Leave and Workplace Flexibility:

One of the most significant areas of progress in father-inclusive policies is the implementation of paternity leave and workplace flexibility. Traditionally, parental leave policies focused primarily on maternity leave, often leaving fathers with limited options for bonding with their newborns. However, research has shown that when fathers take paternity leave, it has profound benefits for both the child and the father. Children experience enhanced cognitive and emotional development, and fathers develop stronger bonds with their children from the outset.

Countries like Norway, Sweden, and Iceland have been pioneers in providing generous paternity leave policies, recognizing the importance of shared parenting responsibilities. These countries offer paid paternity leave, often encouraging fathers to take an equal or significant share of the parental leave period. This approach supports the father's role in the family and promotes gender equality by challenging traditional gender roles.

In addition to paternity leave, workplace flexibility is crucial for supporting fathers. Flexible work hours, remote work options, and policies that accommodate family needs enable fathers to balance their professional responsibilities with their parenting duties. Employers that prioritize work-life balance and provide supportive environments for fathers create a culture where fatherhood is valued and encouraged.

Parenting Programs and Education:

Father-inclusive policies extend beyond the workplace to include parenting programs and educational initiatives. These programs aim to equip fathers with the skills, knowledge, and support they need to be effective parents. Parenting programs specifically tailored for fathers address unique challenges and offer practical advice on child-rearing aspects.

For instance, programs like "Fathers Supporting Fathers" and "Dad Central" in Canada provide resources, workshops, and peer support groups for fathers. These programs create safe spaces where fathers can share their experiences, seek advice, and learn from one another. By fostering a sense of community, these initiatives help fathers feel less isolated and more confident in their parenting abilities.

Educational initiatives also play a vital role in changing societal perceptions of fatherhood. Campaigns that highlight the positive impact of involved fathers challenge stereotypes and encourage more men to embrace active parenting roles. By showcasing diverse examples of fatherhood and celebrating the contributions of fathers, these initiatives promote a more inclusive and supportive culture for all parents.

Legal Reforms and Advocacy:

Legal reforms are essential for creating an equitable framework that supports fathers' involvement. In many countries, custody laws and child support regulations have historically favored mothers, often marginalizing fathers in the process. However, there is a growing recognition of the need for legal systems to be more balanced and father-inclusive.

Advocacy groups and organizations dedicated to fathers' rights work tirelessly to address these legal disparities. They advocate for shared custody arrangements, equitable child support guidelines, and the recognition of fathers' rights in family law. By pushing for reforms that prioritize the best interests of the child while ensuring fair treatment for fathers, these organizations strive to create a more just and inclusive legal landscape.

Community and Social Support:

Community and social support systems are vital for fostering father-inclusive environments. Community centers, faith-based organizations, and social service agencies can play a significant role in providing resources and support for fathers. These organizations offer parenting classes, support groups, and recreational activities that promote father-child bonding.

For example, organizations like the "Father's Club" in the United States create spaces where fathers can come together, share their experiences, and participate in activities with children, fellow fathers, and the community. These community-driven efforts help fathers build strong networks and gain valuable insights into effective parenting and community development.

Media and Cultural Representation:

Media and cultural representation are powerful tools for shaping perceptions of fatherhood. Positive portrayals of fathers in television shows, movies, literature, and advertising can challenge stereotypes and highlight the diverse roles fathers play in their families. When fathers are depicted as caring, competent, and actively involved, it reinforces the message that fatherhood is valuable and essential.

Media campaigns that celebrate fatherhood, such as the "Dads Matter" campaign, emphasize the importance of father involvement and encourage society to appreciate the contributions of fathers. By normalizing active and engaged fatherhood, these campaigns inspire more men to embrace their roles as fathers and take pride in their parenting responsibilities.

The development of father-inclusive policies and practices is necessary for supporting and encouraging active fatherhood. By implementing paternity leave, workplace flexibility, parenting programs, legal reforms, community support, and positive media representation, we can create an environment where fathers are valued and empowered. These initiatives not only benefit fathers and children but also contribute to a more equitable and inclusive society. By recognizing and celebrating the vital role of fathers, we can ensure that all children have the opportunity to thrive in loving and supportive families.

Fatherhood is a dynamic and evolving role enriched by diverse cultural perspectives, alternative family structures, and supportive policies. By recognizing and embracing these variations, the creation of a more inclusive environment that honors the unique contributions of fathers becomes possible. From paternity leave to community programs, these initiatives empower fathers to be active, involved, and nurturing, ultimately benefiting children and society as a whole. As one continues to champion father-inclusive practices, they pave the way for stronger families and more resilient communities, making sure that fatherhood is honored and supported in all its diverse forms.

Chapter 14: Personal Stories of Fatherhood

Over the course of time, the concept of fatherhood has undergone significant changes and is brimmed with many stories of fathers standing up to its true meaning. Where the negative stories of abusive or uncaring fathers exist, true patriots of fatherhood have adorned this concept with their dedication to their children, and even today, they shine as role models for fathers around the world.

Before delving into the stories of those fathers, the impact of having a father around needs to be clarified. For instance, in my experience, I was raised by a single parent and grew up without a father, not learning who or where he was until I reached adulthood. Lacking a father's presence or male guidance, I made many decisions independently, without outside influence. My mother, who was young and lacked strong parental skills due to her own upbringing, did her best, but it was a challenging journey. The absence of a father often means there is no male to offer guidance, support, or leadership, which can often lead to challenging circumstances.

Children without a father figure can make misguided choices, sometimes resulting in legal troubles. Mothers can become overwhelmed and might struggle to discipline effectively, allowing kids to act out and potentially engage in criminal behavior. While I turned out well without a father, I recognize that having a nurturing and supportive father could have provided valuable guidance. However, the mere presence of a man in the home isn't a solution—an abusive or toxic father can worsen a child's situation.

It's not a guarantee that two-parent households are better. Effective parenting depends on the individuals involved. Children learn from their parents' actions, whether positive or negative. So, whether in a single-parent or dual-parent household, what matters most is the quality of parenting and the environment created. Good people can come from single-parent homes, and bad people can come from two-parent homes. It's not always straightforward.

Despite the challenges, my journey taught me the profound importance of positive fatherhood. The absence of a father in my life underscored how crucial it is for fathers to be present and engaged. Fathers who provide love, support, and guidance can shape their children's futures in powerful ways. They offer a sense of security and a model for responsible, caring behavior. The potential impact of a father's involvement is immense, inspiring children to overcome obstacles and strive for a better future. Let us gain insight by learning from the examples of these fathers – men who embodied the true essence of fatherhood.

Inspirational Father-figures:

Jim Redmond:

In the 1992 Barcelona Olympics, Derek Redmond, a British sprinter, was a favorite to win a medal in the 400 meters (Derek Redmond, 2024). He had trained relentlessly for this moment, overcoming previous injuries and setbacks. As the race began, Derek surged ahead with determination, his dreams of Olympic glory within reach. But as he rounded the backstretch, disaster struck. Derek's hamstring snapped, and he fell to the track in agony.

At that moment, the world seemed to stop. Derek, writhing in pain, watched as his competitors raced past him. His Olympic dream appeared shattered. But what happened next turned a moment of despair into one of the most inspirational displays of fatherly love and support ever witnessed.

From the stands, Jim Redmond saw his son's anguish. He pushed past security and ran onto the track, determined to be by Derek's side. As he reached Derek, Jim gently lifted his son to his feet. "You don't have to do this," Jim told him, but Derek insisted, "Yes, I do." With tears in their eyes, father and son began to walk together, step by step, toward the finish line.

The crowd, initially silent in shock, began to roar with applause and encouragement. Jim's presence gave Derek the strength to continue. They leaned on each other, Derek hobbling in pain but refusing to give up. Jim's arm around his son was a symbol of the love and support that had defined their relationship. Together, they completed the lap, crossing the finish line to a standing ovation.

Jim Redmond's actions that day epitomized the essence of fatherhood. His willingness to step in and support his son in his darkest moment demonstrated a father's unyielding commitment to his child's well-being. Jim didn't care about the rules or the officials; his only concern was for his son's emotional and physical pain.

Jim's story serves as a testament to the power of a father's love. It shows that being a father is not limited to providing for a child but also about being there in their times of need, offering strength when they feel weak, and encouraging them to persevere in the face of adversity. Jim Redmond's actions were an embodiment of hope and inspiration for countless people worldwide, reminding us of the profound impact a father can have on his child's life.

In the years that followed, Derek Redmond spoke often about that day and the crucial role his father played. He highlighted how his father's support had always been a cornerstone of his life, not just in that moment on the track but throughout his entire journey. Jim Redmond's unwavering belief in his son and willingness to stand by him no matter the circumstances are a powerful reminder that true fatherhood is about being present, supportive, and a source of strength and encouragement.

Jim Redmond's story is an enigmatic example of the lengths to which fathers will and should go to support their children. It reminds us that the greatest victories are not always measured by medals or accolades but by the love, support, and guidance that fathers provide.

Dwayne Wade:

Dwyane Wade's journey as a father is an inspiring testament to the transformative power of love, commitment, and resilience. Beyond his storied career in the NBA, Wade's most profound legacy may well be the way he has embraced and excelled in the role of a father.

Wade's story begins in the challenging environment of the South Side of Chicago, where he faces numerous obstacles. Yet, it was his role as a father that became his true calling. After a highly publicized legal battle, Wade took full custody of his two sons, Zaire and Zion, demonstrating extraordinary dedication and selflessness. Balancing the demands of an elite basketball career with parenting responsibilities, Wade showed that being a present, engaged father was his highest priority.

Countless times, he highlighted the impactful role his own father played in his life. At the 2023 Naismith Memorial Basketball Hall of Fame enshrinement ceremony (Brown, 2023), Dwayne gave a speech – addressing his father:

"I owe you a debt of gratitude that I'll never be able to repay. When I would cry and say, 'I can't,' you made me go harder. You pushed me to the limits I didn't know were inside of me [and] the hard work I put in was because I didn't want to let you down. Even though I hated being called 'Little Dwyane,' I admired you as a kid. I admire you now..."

Brought up under the influence of a good father, he understood the values of the role fatherhood carried within it. His commitment to his children went beyond mere presence. Wade actively involved Zaire and Zion in his world, from attending games to participating in charitable endeavors. This level of involvement was not just about sharing experiences but about creating lasting memories and imparting life lessons. Wade's approach was deeply rooted in the belief that family comes first, and he consistently made choices that prioritized their well-being and growth.

One of the most inspirational aspects of Wade's fatherhood is his unwavering support for his daughter, Zaya, who came out as transgender. Wade's acceptance and advocacy for Zaya highlight his profound understanding of what it means to truly support and nurture a child. He publicly celebrated Zaya's identity, demonstrating an extraordinary level of love and respect. His stance on this issue has not only influenced his family but has also served as a beacon of acceptance and understanding for many.

Wade's dedication to fatherhood extends to his philanthropic efforts as well. Through the Dwyane Wade Foundation, he has worked tirelessly to create opportunities for underserved youth, reflecting his belief in the power of giving back. His commitment to using his platform for positive change is a testament to the values he instills in his children.

Dwyane Wade's role as a father is a powerful reminder of the impact one individual can have through love, dedication, acceptance, and selflessness. His story is a celebration of how fatherhood can transform lives, not just within the family but in the wider community.

Wade's example shows that being a father means more than just providing; it means actively engaging, supporting, and advocating for one's children. His legacy as a father is a profound testament to the power of love and commitment in shaping not just a family but the world around us.

Richard Williams:

Richard Williams' journey as a father is a compelling testament to the power of unwavering belief and relentless dedication. His story is not simply about the triumphs of his daughters, Venus and Serena, but also about the remarkable role he played in their lives—a role marked by profound love, sacrifice, and vision.

Growing up in the segregated South, Richard Williams faced the harsh realities of racial discrimination and economic hardship. Despite these obstacles, he harbored a bold dream for his daughters—one that transcended the limitations of his own circumstances. He saw in them the potential to break barriers and redefine the game of tennis. With no formal training in the sport, only the lessons he took from a man known as "Old Whiskey," Williams crafted a detailed plan of about 85 pages to guide his daughters from a young age, driven by a deep-seated belief in their capabilities and his unshakable resolve (Richard Williams (Tennis Coach), 2024).

Richard's approach to parenting was characterized by an extraordinary mix of strict discipline and unconditional support. He designed rigorous training regimens and set high expectations but also ensured that his daughters felt cherished and encouraged. His presence in their lives was not just as a coach but a constant source of emotional strength and practical wisdom, instilling in them values of resilience, determination, and self-belief.

His role extended beyond the tennis court. Richard Williams was a father who prioritized his daughters' well-being and future above all else. He moved his family to Compton, California, a decision made not for convenience but to provide them with opportunities that were otherwise out of reach. His commitment was visible in every aspect of their lives, from managing their training schedules to handling the pressures of professional tennis.

The fruits of his labor are undeniable. Venus and Serena Williams have become icons across the world for their athletic achievements and their ability to overcome systemic barriers and challenge stereotypes. Their success is a direct reflection of Richard's sacrifices and his unwavering dedication. He showed the world that with love, vision, and perseverance, a father could shape the lives of his children in profound and extraordinary ways.

Richard Williams' story is an inspiring example of how fatherhood, when driven by compassion and determination, can forge a path to greatness. His legacy is not just in the trophies and titles his daughters have won but in the unwavering belief he had in them, the sacrifices he made, and the values he instilled. His journey underscores that the role of a father is transformative, capable of turning dreams into reality and empowering children to rise above their circumstances.

Just as Richard saw potential where others saw obstacles, every father can discover hidden talents in their children. With patience, dedication, and love, you can help them reach their full potential. Remember, you're not just raising a child but building a future leader, a compassionate individual, and a lifelong friend.

Team Hoyt:

In the gallery of praiseworthy fatherhood icons, few are as moving and motivational as that of Team Hoyt—Dick and Rick

Hoyt. Their journey is a testament to the limitless bounds of a father's love and dedication.

Rick Hoyt was born in 1962 with cerebral palsy, a condition that left him unable to walk or speak. The doctors suggested institutionalizing Rick, claiming he would live a life with little to no hope of a "normal" existence. But Dick Hoyt and his wife Judy refused to accept this fate for their son. They saw Rick's potential, intelligence, and spirit and were determined to give him the best life possible (Our Inspiration, n.d.).

As Rick grew, his parents fought to integrate him into everyday activities, ensuring he attended public schools. Rick's breakthrough came when engineers at Tufts University built an interactive computer that allowed him to communicate. One day, Rick told his father that he wanted to participate in a five-mile benefit run for a lacrosse player who had been paralyzed in an accident. Dick, who was not a runner, decided he would push Rick in his wheelchair for the race.

That first race was a revelation. After they crossed the finish line, Rick told his father, "Dad, when I'm running, it feels like I'm not handicapped." This simple yet profound statement was the spark that ignited a lifelong partnership known as Team Hoyt.

What followed was nothing short of remarkable. Dick began training, carrying bags of cement and running, building his stamina and strength as he couldn't practice with Rick since he attended school at that time. Shortly after, they started participating in countless races, from marathons to triathlons. They faced each challenge head-on, with Dick pushing Rick's wheelchair during the running segments, pulling him in a specially designed boat during the swimming segments, and carrying him in a seat attached to a bicycle during the cycling segments. Their perseverance, resilience, and teamwork were awe-inspiring.

One of their most notable achievements was completing the Ironman Triathlon in Hawaii, a grueling event that includes a 2.4-mile swim, a 112-mile bike ride, and a 26.2-mile marathon. Completing such an arduous event is a formidable task for any athlete, but Dick did it all while supporting his son, proving the extraordinary strength of a father's love and determination.

The Hoyts' story is not just about athletic achievement; it is about the unyielding bond between a father and son. It's about a father who saw beyond his son's physical limitations and nurtured his potential, helping him experience life to its fullest. Through their races, Dick gave Rick the freedom and joy that his physical condition had taken away. They shared a connection that transcended words communicated through every mile they conquered together.

The impact of Team Hoyt extends far beyond their personal achievements. Their story has touched the hearts of millions around the world, inspiring people to overcome their own challenges and to see beyond disabilities to the potential within. It is a powerful reminder of what can be accomplished with love, determination, and unwavering support.

Dick Hoyt's dedication to his son teaches us that fatherhood is about more than biological ties—it's about commitment, sacrifice, and unconditional love. His example shows that the most profound achievements are those driven by the heart. The legacy of Team Hoyt continues to inspire and remind us that with love and perseverance, anything is possible. Rick's father, Dick Hoyt's words about his son, adorn the concept of fatherhood, and for eternity, as long as fatherhood exists, they will remain vivid to every father on the planet.

"He's the one who has motivated me because if it wasn't for him, I wouldn't be out there doing triathlons. What I'm doing is loaning Rick my arms and legs so he can be out there competing like everybody else."

~ Dick Hoyt

Diverse Fatherhood Experiences:

In a world where family dynamics and structure are increasingly diverse, the experiences of fatherhood in such contexts offer valuable lessons on inclusion and understanding. When we talk about mixed or biracial families, we encounter a unique set of dynamics and opportunities. These families often include parents from different racial or cultural backgrounds, each bringing their own traditions, values, and ways of raising children.

One key challenge in these diverse households is finding a balance between the different cultural influences. For instance, a biracial child with a Black mother and a White father might be exposed to two distinct sets of cultural practices and beliefs. Each parent may have their own vision of how they want their child to be raised based on their upbringing and experiences. This situation can create a challenge when it comes to integrating both cultural perspectives into the child's life.

The essence of fatherhood in such diverse contexts lies in the ability to harmonize these different influences. It requires an intentional effort to blend the cultural elements in a way that honors both parents' backgrounds while providing the child with a rich, multidimensional identity. This blending of cultures doesn't mean choosing one over the other but rather creating an environment where both can coexist and be appreciated.

In practice, this might involve celebrating various cultural holidays, incorporating traditions from both sides and educating the child about the significance of their mixed heritage. It's not just about presenting different viewpoints but nurturing an environment where the child feels valued and understood from both cultural perspectives. This approach helps children develop a well-rounded understanding of their identity and the world around them.

Moreover, such experiences teach us the broader lesson of inclusivity. As diverse families strive to integrate various cultural elements, the same principles can apply to our broader societal interactions. Embracing diversity and inclusion within the family helps set the foundation for children to appreciate and respect differences in others. It instills a sense of empathy and understanding that transcends personal experiences and contributes to a more inclusive society.

Navigating fatherhood in a diverse family setting is about encouraging an environment where multiple cultural narratives are acknowledged and valued. It's a lesson in balance, respect, and the beauty of diversity, shaping children who grow up with a profound appreciation and respect for the true beauty of human experience.

Conclusion

As we close this exploration of fatherhood, it's essential to reflect on the heart of our journey: the profound impact fathers have on their children and the dynamic role they play across various contexts. This book has examined fatherhood from multiple angles, shedding light on both the challenges and triumphs that come with this vital role. Fatherhood transcends mere participation; it is an active, evolving journey that shapes not only the lives of children but the very fabric of our society.

We began by defining what it means to be a father in today's world, recognizing the pivotal influence a father has on his child's development. From the early historical perspectives to modern-day expectations, we've observed how the role of fatherhood has transformed. These changes reflect a deeper understanding of the complex dynamics of family life and the evolving needs of children. This journey is more than about fulfilling traditional roles; it's about embracing a vision where fathers are active, engaged, and present in ways that encourage growth, stability, and love.

Throughout this book, we have explored the range of benefits of an involved father—how emotional support, cognitive guidance, and social interactions contribute to a child's well-being. The challenges faced by fathers, from societal expectations to balancing professional and personal lives – of both in relationship and single fathers, have been examined with empathy and practical insight. Each chapter has highlighted strategies and stories that underscore the strength and resilience required to navigate these hurdles.

We've looked into how fathers influence their children's identity, educational achievements, and emotional health. The narratives we shared illustrate that the positive impacts of fatherhood extend beyond mere existence; they shape futures, build character, and instill values. Strengthening father-child bonds through effective communication, active involvement, and positive discipline is not just a goal—it's a commitment to nurturing future generations with love and integrity.

As we examined fatherhood across different cultural and global contexts, we peeked into a richer perspective on the diverse ways fathers contribute to their children's lives. These stories and experiences offer powerful lessons on inclusivity, adaptability, and the universal truths that unite all fathers.

As society changes and people's lifestyles evolve, today's family may include parents of the same gender raising children. Unfortunately, such couples are rigorously scrutinized by society without considering how it might impact their mental health. While traditional views of mother and father roles may shift, the essence of parenthood remains the same. For children, their parents are symbols of hope and role models they can look up to. Society should acknowledge and understand that the true essence of parenting is not defined by gender but by the nurturing love and support provided by the parents. Regardless of gender similarity, both parents can share responsibilities and maintain a strong presence in their children's lives. However, in our evolving society, many still struggle to accept same-gender parenting.

As a result, many children face taunts and abuse in their social circles for having parents of the same gender. These issues need to be addressed with an understanding of the times we live in rather than radicalizing people over their preferences. Children still need guidance, support, development, and love. The genders of those fulfilling these roles should not matter as long as the children's needs are met.

In closing, it's vital to embrace the profound message of this book: fatherhood is not defined by perfection but by the dedication to being present, engaged, and supportive. The journey of fatherhood is one of continuous growth and learning, where every effort, no matter how small, makes a significant difference.

Let this be a call to action for all fathers—whether you're stepping into the role for the first time or navigating its evolving demands. Embrace the challenges with courage and the rewards with pride. Your role is more than a title; it is a commitment to shaping lives, building futures, and creating a legacy of love and support.

May you draw inspiration from the diverse experiences shared, and may they empower you to approach fatherhood with renewed passion and purpose. Together, let's nurture a world where every father is supported in his journey, and every child benefits from the nurturing presence of a dedicated father. The future is bright, and it begins with the impactful choices we make today.

"Fatherhood is not about being perfect; it's about being present. It's in the everyday acts of love and dedication that you leave a lasting legacy. The love and guidance you impart shape the future more than you can ever imagine."

References

What Is Fatherhood? 11 Great Dads Outline What Fatherhood Means To Them – Daily Dad – The Blog. (n.d.). https://dailydad.com/what-is-fatherhood/

A Brief History of Fatherhood. (2015, June 17). Superpages. https://www.superpages.com/em/brief-history-fatherhood/

Why fathers are important role models for boys. (2013, June 13). Psychologymum. https://psychologymum.wordpress.com/2013/06/13/why-fathers-are-important-role-models-for-boys/

Harker, J. (2019, March 6). Father figures: why the new wave of visible black dads gives me hope (The Guardian, Ed.) [Review of Father figures: why the new wave of visible black dads gives me hope]. The Guardian. https://www.theguardian.com/lifeandstyle/2019/mar/06/father-figures-why-the-new-wave-of-visible-black-dads-give-me-hope

A Father's Impact on Child Development. (2018, June 7). Child Abuse Prevention, Treatment & Welfare Services | Children's Bureau. https://www.all4kids.org/news/blog/a-fathers-impact-on-child-development/#:~:text=High%20levels%20of%20father%20involvement

Kim, S., & Glasgow, A. E. (2018). The effect of father's absence, parental adverse events, and neighborhood disadvantage on children's aggression and delinquency: A multi-analytic approach. Journal of Human Behavior in the Social Environment, 28(5), 570–587. https://doi.org/10.1080/10911359.2018.1443866

BlackPast. (2007, January 21). (1965) The Moynihan Report: The Negro Family, the Case for National Action • BlackPast. BlackPast.

https://www.blackpast.org/african-american-history/moynihan-report-1965/

LBJ's "War on Poverty" Hurt Black Americans. (2014, January 8). https://nationalcenter.org/ncppr/2014/01/08/lbjs-war-on-poverty-hurt-black-americans/

The Ways Fathers Impact Child Development | Celebree School. (2022, June 14). Www.celebree.com. https://www.celebree.com/the-ways-fathers-impact-child-development/#:~:text=Studies%20have%20consistently%20shown%20that

Importance of Fathers & Statistics | A Father's Place - A Father's Place. (n.d.). Www.afathersplace.org. https://www.afathersplace.org/why-it-matters/fathers/#:~:text=Research%20shows%20that%20when%20fathers

Bagattini, A. (2019). Children's well-being and vulnerability. Ethics and Social Welfare, 13(3), 211–215. https://doi.org/10.1080/17496535.2019.1647973

Bethune, S. (2014). Teen stress rivals that of adults. American Psychological Association. https://www.apa.org/monitor/2014/04/teen-stress

Lamb, Pleck, Lerner, & Steinberg. (2002). ADOLESCENT PSYCHOLOGY [Review of ADOLESCENT PSYCHOLOGY]. Al-Edu. https://www.al-edu.com/wp-content/uploads/2014/05/LernerSteinberg-eds-Handbook-of-Adolescent-Psychology.pdf

Centers for Disease Control and Prevention. (2023). Data and Statistics on Children's Mental Health. Centers for Disease Control and Prevention; CDC. https://www.cdc.gov/childrensmentalhealth/data.html

Father Involvement Statistics • WorldMetrics. (2024, May 5). https://worldmetrics.org/father-involvement-statistics/

The Modern Families Index 2017. (n.d.). Retrieved June 4, 2024, from https://workingfamilies.org.uk/wp-content/uploads/2017/01/Modern-Families-Index_Full-Report.pdf

Breivik, K., & Olweus, D. (2006). Adolescent's Adjustment in Four Post-Divorce Family Structures: Single Mother, Single Father, Stepfather, and Stepmother Families. Journal of Divorce & Remarriage, 44(3-4), 99-124.

Gershoff, E. T. (2013). Spanking and Child Development: We Know Enough Now to Stop Hitting Our Children. Child Development Perspectives, 7(3), 133-137.

Hentges, R. F., Shaw, D. S., Wang, M., & Kurtz, M. (2018). Developmental trajectories of parental discipline and adolescent adjustment. Journal of Abnormal Child Psychology, 46(4), 663-675.

Zolotor, A. J., Theodore, A. D., Chang, J. J., Berkoff, M. C., & Runyan, D. K. (2008). Speak softly—and forget the stick: Corporal punishment and child physical abuse. American Journal of Preventive Medicine, 35(4), 364-369.

Benedikt Brüning. (2020, May 7). Ikumen -The new fathering in Japan: How do organizations and governmental reforms in family policy affect... ResearchGate; unknown. https://www.researchgate.net/publication/345894748_Ikumen_-The_new_fathering_in_Japan_How_do_organizations_and_governmental_reforms_in_family_policy_affect_the_involvement_of_Japanese_fathers_in_parenting

Seward, R., Ray, Rush, M., & Anthony, M. (n.d.). Title Fathers, Fathering, and Fatherhood across Cultures: Convergence or Divergence? https://researchrepository.ucd.ie/server/api/core/bitstreams

Derek Redmond. (2024, July 15). Wikipedia. https://en.wikipedia.org/wiki/Derek_Redmond#:~:text=due%20to%20injuries.-

Our Inspiration. (n.d.). Retrieved July 25, 2024, from https://teamhoytsd.com/about-us-2/

Brown, P. (2023, August 14). Dwyane Wade Honors His Father In Heartwarming Hall Of Fame Speech. VIBE.com. https://www.vibe.com/news/sports/dwyane-wade-father-hall-of-fame-acceptance-speech-1234780177/

Richard Williams (tennis coach). (2024, July 16). Wikipedia. https://en.wikipedia.org/wiki/Richard_Williams_(tennis_coach)#cite_note-6